Six SIGMA Green Belt Study Guide 2019

Six SIGMA Exam Preparation and Practice Test Questions

Six Sigma Green Belt Essential Test Tips DVD

from Trivium Test Prep!

Dear Customer,

Thank you for purchasing from Trivium Test Prep! We're honored to help you prepare for your Six Sigma Green Belt.

To show our appreciation, we're offering a **FREE *Six Sigma Green Belt Essential Test Tips* DVD by Trivium Test Prep**. Our DVD includes 35 test preparation strategies that will make you successful on the Six Sigma Green Belt. All we ask is that you email us your feedback and describe your experience with our product. Amazing, awful, or just so-so: we want to hear what you have to say!

To receive your **FREE *Six Sigma Green Belt Essential Test Tips* DVD**, please email us at 5star@triviumtestprep.com. Include "Free 5 Star" in the subject line and the following information in your email:

1. The title of the product you purchased.

2. Your rating from 1 – 5 (with 5 being the best).

3. Your feedback about the product, including how our materials helped you meet your goals and ways in which we can improve our products.

4. Your full name and shipping address so we can send your FREE *Six Sigma Green Belt Essential Test Tips* DVD.

If you have any questions or concerns please feel free to contact us directly at 5star@triviumtestprep.com.

Thank you!

Table of Contents

y due to its applicability to most any business or industry. Companies realize the

ıution, invest wisely in your choice of certification provider. A potential custome

will sell you a greenbelt certification today for $19.95. The certificate is only as

utable providers will have the following basic requirements for experience and/oı

100 multiple-choice question examination typically four hours in length

xpectations for a Certified Six Sigma Green Belt are that they demonstrate knowledge of Six Sigma tools and processes, are involved in quality improvement projects, and analyze and solve quality problems.

The information that follows composes the Body of Knowledge for the Six Sigma Green Belt Certification in general content and topical areas. As the ASQ is the preeminent source for six sigma certification the subject matter of the BOK mirrors theirs most closely.

Overview: Six Sigma and the Organization (15 Questions)

Six sigma and organizational goals

Six Sigma is an improvement methodology which uses the stages of Define, Measure, Analyze, Improve, and Control to make improvements. "Six Sigma" measures the capability of a process to perform defect free work with a failure rate of 3.4 parts per million or 99.9997%. The Six Sigma methodology uses proven strategies, tools, and statistical methodologies to improve the

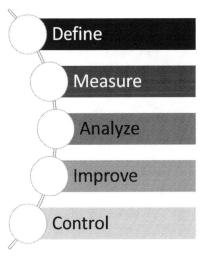

financial bottom line of companies. The goal of Six Sigma is to improve profits through variability and defect reduction, improved process performance, and increased customer satisfaction through consistent services, products, or processes.

- The **define** phase determines what problem needs to be solved
- The **measure** phase determines the capabilities of processes
- The **analyze** phase includes determining where problems or defects occur
- The **improve** phase determines how processes can be improved and implement trials of solutions
- The **control** phase determines what can be put into place to sustain the improvements made

Six Sigma reduces costs and waste by determining the Cost of Poor Quality. The process a Green Belt or six sigma project will take is summarized in these basic steps:

1. Understand who your customers are and what is important to them.

2. Understand customer feedback through the Voice of the Customer and determine the requirements for your product.

3. Prioritize issues related to your product.

4. Determine internal processes and what causes variation.

5. Determine the causes of defects.

6. Develop ways to address the defects.

7. Develop metrics to standardize and measure the changes made in the process.

The Six Sigma Body of Knowledge is similar to the Project Management Body of Knowledge (PMBOK). There are inherent characteristics you will have as a greenbelt and this is the body of knowledge which provides the skillset necessary for a green belt to perform process improvement.

Certification begins with an understanding of recognized process improvement programs such as Total Quality Management and the International Standards Organization then factors such as common cause and special cause variation, waste reduction and elimination, DMAIC and design for Six Sigma Models. Then important leaders in Six Sigma including Shewart, Deming, Juran, Baldrige, Taguchi, Goldratt, and Ishikawa.

The core knowledge consists of basic process improvement, Cost of Quality and Cost of Poor Quality, Cost Benefit Analysis, Return on Investment, Sigma Levels and Gauge R&R. Industry Benchmarking and or Metrics, and Six Sigma Tools such as flowcharting, histogram, pareto chart, scatter diagrams, control charts, value stream mapping, and fishbone analysis.

Basic DMAIC activities at each level include:

- **Define** core activities include the project charter, scope, deliverables, process map, cost benefit analysis, and stakeholders analysis.
- **Measure** core activities include measurement systems analysis, benchmarking, return on investment calculations, failure mode and effects analysis, and Gauge R&R.
- **Analyze** core activities include analyze data, determine root causes, determine correlations, mean, mode, median, variance, variation, and correlation as well as hypothesis testing and design of experiments.
- **Improve** core activities include determine 3-5 solutions, pilot solutions, and roll out solutions.
- **Control** core activities include the control plan and control chart.

Pre DMAIC or Pre -DFSS activities include activities such as developing the Strengths, Weakness, Opportunity, and Threats, (SWOT) model.

Project management responsibilities may include constraint management, implementation techniques including risk management, project leadership, and project planning. Additional skills may include team building, use of project management tools, conflict management and negotiation tactics and determine the Voice of the Customer and Voice of the Process.

In general Green Belts are trained to implement Six Sigma projects and they carry out these activities along with their regular responsibilities. Green Belts spend around 25 to 50 percent of their time involved in the Six Sigma projects. They are aware of all the activities involved in the business process.

Greenbelts should be able to explain the importance of the y equals a function of x formula to the business and the processes. Greenbelts are trained in the DMAIC model and in using various tools needed to carry out the data collection and for validating the measurement system.

Value of six sigma

Under the value of six sigma the greenbelt candidate should recognize why organizations use six sigma, how they apply its philosophy and goals, and the origins of six sigma.

The Six Sigma Methodology is one of the most popular business improvement practices used today. The Motorola Corporation which produces wireless infrastructure and provides mission-critical communications, products, and services to enterprises and governments is credited with creating and implementing this methodology in the mid 1980's.

A multitude of quality control methods have come and gone such as Total Quality Management (TQM) or (TQMS) but Six Sigma methodology is the most popular proven method it complements many certifications of the International Standards Organization such as ISO 9000 or 9001 which provide standards for quality management systems. Plan, do, study, act (PDSA), Taguchi Methods, business process engineering, and international standards are common initiatives all of which have contributed to improving quality.

Six Sigma systems have been implemented in a multitude of major corporations with substantial results. Between 1986 and 2001 Motorola estimates that through implementation of six sigma processes they have accrued savings of over $16 billion. Honeywell reports for 1998 to 2000 a savings of $1.8 billion, Ford Motor Company reported $1 billion, and General Electric reported $12 billion in a five year period. They saved money by reducing repair times, reducing order delays, reducing defects, increasing customer satisfaction, increasing productivity, and decreasing measurement error. Six Sigma can be described as working Smarter not Harder.

Six Sigma can be defined in a statistical manner too. The sigma symbol represents standard deviations from the normal range in a business process. The more deviation, the less desirable a product is. A Six Sigma business process is a process in which defective parts per million opportunities (DPMO) are determined and refined.

- At the Six Sigma level a business process produces only 3.4 defects per million opportunities.
- At the 5th Sigma level 233 defective parts per million occur.
- At the 4th Sigma level 6,210 defective parts per million occur.
- At the 3rd Sigma level 66,807 defective parts per million occur.
- At the 2nd Sigma level 308,538 defective parts per million occur.

Quality improvement has been needed since businesses began and it has evolved through history into a highly refined system and methodology to improve quality. Six Sigma is the result of bits and pieces of many individuals' contributions to the quality movement.

Quality and Six Sigma History

The word sigma has been used for years by mathematicians and engineers as a symbol for a unit of measurement of variation called standard deviation. The quality initiative history developed significantly at the beginning of the 1900's but has some origins even further back in history such as **Carl Frederick Gauss** (1777-1855) who was the first scientist to introduce the normal curve. Historically important was the understanding of deviation.

Walter Shewart explained how three sigma or three standard deviations is where a process needs to be corrected. This is the point where a product will need to be remade because it will not pass a quality inspection.

The next individuals created significant works and bodies of knowledge which enhanced and developed the quality movement.

Dr. W. Edwards Deming (1900–1993) is best known for reminding management that most problems are systemic and that it is management's responsibility to improve the systems so that workers can do their jobs more effectively.

Deming argued that higher quality leads to higher productivity, which, in turn, leads to long-term competitive strength. The theory is that improvements in quality lead to lower costs and higher productivity because they result in less rework, fewer mistakes, fewer delays, and better use of time and materials. Deming taught quality and productivity improvement for more than fifty years. He noted that **workers are responsible for 10 to 20 percent of the quality problems in a factory, and that the remaining 80 to 90 percent is under management's control**. He emphasized cooperation of workers and management to achieve high-quality products.

Deming's theories were taught as a part of his System of Profound Knowledge. His knowledge system consists of four interrelated parts: **(1) Theory of Optimization; (2) Theory of Variation; (3) Theory of Knowledge; and (4) Theory of Psychology**. In the theory of optimization. The objective of an organization is the optimization of the total system and not the optimization of the individual subsystems. In the theory of variation. Deming's philosophy focuses on improving the product and service uncertainty and variability in design and manufacturing processes. In the theory of knowledge. Deming emphasized that knowledge is not possible without theory, and experience alone does not establish a theory. He says copying a best practice without understanding the theory behind it could be devastating for a company.
In the theory of psychology. Psychology helps to understand people, interactions between people and circumstances, interactions between leaders and employees in a system of management.

Deming wanted to transform management and began teaching his 14 points.

	Deming's 14 Points
1	Establish constancy of purpose: plan and manage to the plan; detect and correct deviations.
2	Improve constantly and forever every system of production and service: small continuous improvement is better than infrequent quantum leaps.
3	Eliminate numerical goals and quotas including management by objective: unsupported arbitrary objectives can be both restrictive and demoralizing.
4	Eliminate fear so that everyone may work effectively for the Company: mistakes happen and fear of disclosure impedes correction.
5	Institute leadership: managers must not be cops or directors but rather coaches of the creative team.
6	End the practice of awarding business largely on the basis of price: product quality, product improvement, and reliability of supply are important.
7	Break down the barriers between departments: encourage communication and cooperation – eliminate chimneys and silos.
8	Institute training on the job: as product and process content grows, not all employees come equally prepared.
9	Eliminate the annual rating or merit system: performance is subject to variation whereas shared reward develops teamwork.
10	Institute a vigorous program of education and self-improvement: as employees promote the company, the company must develop its employees.
11	Eliminate slogans and exhortations: management, not an individual worker, is responsible for system performance.
12	Cease dependence on mass inspection: it is impractical to sort quality into a system that produces bad product.
13	Adopt the new philosophy: every department of the company can quantitatively measure its output.
14	Create a structure in top management to accomplish the transformation: successful systems can only be introduced and maintained by top management.

The Deming Cycle known as **Plan-Do-Check-Act PDCA Cycle or Plan-Do-Study-Act PDCA** was invented by **Shewhart** and popularized by Deming. This is a cyclic process approach for planning and testing improvement activities prior to full-scale implementation.

The steps in the Deming PDCA or PDSA Cycle are:
1. Plan a change or test **P.**
2. Do it **D**. Carry out the change or test, preferably on a small scale.
3. Check it **C**. Observe the effects of the change or test.
4. Study it **S**.
5. Act on what was learned **A**.
6. Repeat and continuously evaluate

Joseph Juran was born in 1904 in Braila, Romania. He was a quality professional who worked in the inspection branch of the Hawthorne Co. of Western Electric. He worked with the U. S. government during World War II and afterward became a quality consultant. In 1952, Dr. Juran was invited to Japan. Dr. Edward Deming helped arrange the meeting that led to this invitation and his many years of work with Japanese companies. Juran founded the Juran Center for Quality Improvement at the University of Minnesota and the Juran Institute.

He developed the quality trilogy which emphasized the roles of quality planning, quality control, and quality improvement.

Dr. Genichi Taguchi was a Japanese engineer and statistician who defined what product specification means and how this can be translated into cost effective production. Taguchi's contributions are in robust design in the area of product development. The Taguchi Loss Function, The Taguchi Method (Design of Experiments), and other methodologies have made major contributions in the reduction of variation and greatly improved engineering quality and productivity by reducing environmental variation.

Just in time (JIT) is a production strategy that strives to improve a business return on investment by reducing in-process inventory and associated carrying costs. Taguchi suggests that every process has a target value and that as the product moves away from target value, there's a loss incurred by society. This loss may involve delay, waste, scrap, or rework. This is the Taguchi Loss Function.

Dr. Kaoru Ishikawa (1915–1989) was a professor of engineering at the University of Tokyo and a student of Dr. W. Edwards Deming. He was active in the quality movement in Japan and was awarded the Deming Prize for his writings on quality control. His book Guide to Quality Control 1982 is considered a classic because of its in-depth explanations of quality tools and related statistics. The tool for which he is best known is the cause and effect diagram.

The Six Sigma methodology is not a revolutionary way of thinking but more an evolutionary development in the science of continuous improvement. It uses the best elements from earlier quality initiatives. Good customer service improving business results and processes are not new approaches to business success. Six Sigma provides proven tools, experience, and credibility.

Following is a brief synopsis of the quality movement over the last 100 years:

- In 1798 Eli Whitney introduced mass production and interchangeable parts.
- In 1913 Henry Ford began the moving automobile assembly line and the need for part consistency became more important. It was critical that good parts be available for use so the production assembly line would not be forced to slow down or stop while a worker sorted through piles of parts to find one that fit.

- In 1924 Walter Shewhart introduced a new data collection, display and analysis forming a process control chart and signaling the beginning of the age of statistical quality control.
- In the 1920's quality was driven by inspections.
- In 1950 the U.S. military and the U.S. government required statistically based levels of product quality from its vendors. The military standard MIL-STD-105A was adopted.
- In 1954 Joseph Juran brought his principles of quality management to Japan and helped integrate quality initiatives throughout all layers in organizations. His concept of integration was known as "Big Q" or quality through management's active involvement and ownership.
- In 1973 the Japanese to constantly improve quality and manufacturing capability were more effective than those employed in the United States. Their focus on two aspects of productivity—defect elimination and cycle time reduction—resulted in many significant developments and successes for Toyota and other Japanese companies. In 1980 American manufacturers realized "If Japan Can, Why Can't We"? So we did and companies such as Motorola and GE lead the way.
- 1987 the International Organization for Standardization (ISO) was introduced with a series of quality standards that were adopted by most of the industrialized world to serve as a single global standard.
- In 1987 the US Government introduced the Malcolm Baldrige National Quality Award presented annually by the president and designed to provide an operational definition of business excellence.
- In 1987 Motorola adopted the concepts of Six Sigma shared the new methodology and philosophy with their suppliers, engineers and managers.

1. **Describe how process inputs, outputs, and feedback impact the larger organization.**
   i) **Organizational drivers and metrics**
   ii) **Recognize key drivers for business (profit, market share, customer satisfaction, efficiency, product differentiation) and how key metrics and scorecards are developed and impact the entire organization.**

Each business entity, company or organization has key drivers. These take many forms and are determined by the organization in terms of customer satisfaction, growth, or performance. Each organization should develop the strategic plan using strategic tools such as the SWOT analysis. As the organization determines goals it can develop corresponding metrics to compare its performance. Quite often this is done through industry benchmarking.

Several organizations use the **balanced scorecard** to monitor progress. The balanced scorecard is a management system that provides feedback on both internal business processes and external outcomes to continuously improve strategic performance and results.

The Balanced Scorecard was developed in the early 1990s by Robert Kaplan and David Norton. Kaplan and Norton identified that businesses should determine their strategic direction on more elements than just financial measures alone. They developed a quadrant shaped measure based on customer satisfaction and their performance requirements, financial requirements and performance, business process requirements and measures, and organizational education and growth.

Customer satisfaction is another key measure which is the result of delivering a product or service that meets customer requirements.

Using research and data collection, companies are able to discover all of the problems that are within an organization that may or may not be apparent. The adage "if you don't know about it you can't fix it" holds true.

The six sigma process transforms knowledge and awareness into an opportunity to expand business. Once you realize the problems then you can take action to reduce errors and rework which cost time, opportunities, and money. If quality products and services with little waste are desirable for your business then the Six Sigma methodology is the answer. Improving quality is now seen as a cost of doing business for many managers and is included in annual budgets.

There are four quality ERA's. Looking at the evolution of quality ERA 1 we have an era with little quality which began with salvaging parts, sorting, grading, making corrective actions and corrective actions of identify sources of non-conformance.

- The first era, **ERA 1** of quality was "inspection" the time was the 1800s to early 1900s. The tools used were gauges and other measurement devices, the goal was to detect problems and sort good items from bad. The end result is products may fail and the customer complains.

- In quality **ERA 2** Quality Control begins. This era was during the 1920s to 1950s. The tools used were statistical and mathematical techniques, including process control charts and sampling tables. The goal was to control problems by efficiently sorting good items from bad. Products are designed, manufactured, tested, and rejects are discarded. The results are fewer failing product are distributed but design problems may arise and the customer complains the manufacturer is unhappy about rejects and waste.

- In Quality **ERA 3** Quality Assurance & Good Manufacturing Practices are instituted. In this step products are designed, quality is built into the manufacturing steps. The manufacture is controlled, tested, rejects discarded

The result is fewer product rejects due to manufacturing. The manufacturer is happier, but design problems may still arise and the customer complains.

This ERA was during the 1950s to 1960s. The tools used were cost of quality, total quality control, reliability engineering, and zero defects programs. The goal was to avoid problems through coordinated activities.

- **In ERA 4**, quality is built into design and manufacturing. Manufacture is controlled, tested, and rejects discarded. The results are better designed products which satisfy customers. The manufacturer is happy with fewer rejects and fewer customer complaints.

Using Quality Management Systems, management has greater commitment to and responsibility for establishing effective quality system, providing adequate resources periodically evaluating quality systems, and making changes and adjustments.

1. **Organizational goals and six sigma projects**
   a. **Describe the project selection process including knowing when to use six sigma improvement methodology (DMAIC) as opposed to other problem-solving tools, and confirm that the project supports and is linked to organizational goals.**

Organizations can often meet their goals through a series of projects and performance measure reports. Sometimes projects require more or less time and or skills to complete and sometimes they require additional tools. The tools available under the Six Sigma methodology are endless. A general rule of thumb is that a green belt project or Six Sigma project is one that has a savings of $200,000 or greater to the organization.

Six Sigma projects are used for these general categories or organizational improvements:

- Cost reduction
- Productivity
- Cost avoidance
- Customer satisfaction
- Simplification
- Revenue growth
- Measurement system development
- Infrastructure development
- New products

Here are some of the times when you use Six Sigma:
- Six sigma is used when causes or situations are unknown.
- Complex processes or services with many variables.
- When you need a broad approach with a proven methodology.
- When problems are not well defined.
- When other problem solving tools do not work.

- When the process requires a rigorous testing methodology.

DMAIC and DMADV are both data intensive Six Sigma methodologies used by green and black belts to reduce defects to less than 3.4 per million opportunities. They are both used on business processes. The **DMAIC** model of Define, Measure, Analyze, Improve, and Control is used for products or processes that exist in the organization but do not meet customer specifications or do not perform as designed. The **DMADV** model of Define, Measure, Analyze, Design, and Verify is used for new products or services requiring design and product verification.

Some organizations use other forms of process improvement which are used when a result is needed in a more rapid timeframe or the operation is less complex. **Rapid process improvement workshops (RPIW)** are used for projects only requiring a few weeks or months to complete using short burst sessions where the team defines the problem or process issue, develops a baseline for current systems and processes, identifies operational barriers and failure modes in the current processes, applies Six Sigma and systems engineering principles to redesign current processes to eliminate or mitigate failure modes, designs and implements a pilot test process redesign.

Kaizen is another improvement approach. Kaizen is a Japanese word meaning change for the good popularly known today as continuous improvement. The meaning was initially used as a Japanese philosophy of continuously improving everything we come in contact with during our lifetime. When you refer to Kaizen in your organization it means to improve all facets, functions and processes within your business. Continuously improving standardized systems, processes and support activities improves quality, delivery time, service and cost. Kaizen aims to eliminate waste by elimination of non-value added work.

Lean principles in the organization

Lean principles are a business philosophy of relentlessly eliminating waste to improve and to identify value added activities and ensure that they are performed efficiently and effectively. Lean is a form of continuous improvement attributed to the Toyota Production System (TPS). Although it began as a shop floor philosophy Lean has migrated to office and business environments and has many variations in the way it is applied. The term lean is synonymous with terms "waste reduction", "continuous improvement", or "process improvement". Lean Six Sigma is the combination of Lean and Six Sigma into a single business philosophy. Six sigma is considered a quality tool and lean is an improvement to a process. Both share many of the same tools such as these:

Common Lean tools	• 5S	• Kaizen	• Value stream maps
• Pareto (80/20) charts	• Process flow charts	• Process flow charts	• Kanban
• Poka yoke	• Just In Time Manufacturing	• Countermeasures	• Visual controls

1. **Lean concepts and tools**
   a. **Define and describe concepts such as value chain, flow, pull, perfection, etc., and tools commonly used to eliminate waste, including kaizen, 5S, error-proofing, value-stream mapping, etc.**

The tools of lean are used to make improvements in processes and services. Following are the most common business process terminology:

- The **value chain** is the series of activities that create and build value at every step of a process or service. These are the inputs into the customer's desires.
- **The value stream** is all activities value added and non-value added that are needed to bring a product from raw material state into the state ready for use by a customer or the process to bring a customer requirement from order to delivery and bring a design from concept to launch.
- **Flow** is the progressive achievement of tasks along the value stream so a product proceeds from design to launch with no stoppages, scrap or backflows. This covers order placement to delivery of a product or service in any business.
- **Pull** system replaces items as they are withdrawn used to avoid push. This involves flowing product in small batches, pacing the processes to stop overproduction, signaling replenishment via signals and leveling the product mix and quantity over time.
- **Perfection** is a state of quality where a product or process is complete and the customer has no additional wants for improvement of the product or service.
- **Kanban** uses a system of signal cards that is simple and shows someone that something in a process needs attention. It is derived from the combination of two Japanese words, kan – (visual) and ban – (card). Kanban roughly translates to sign board or signal board. Kanban is a process of manufacturing or work space organization that relies upon visual signals to control inventory. It was developed by Toyota and Taiichi Ohno, during the late 1940s and early 1950s. During that period, the Toyota Corporation studied American supermarkets and their management techniques. They noticed the relationship between inventory and logistics in the supermarkets such as an empty bin of oranges or lack of canned food on an aisle. The premise behind Kanban is a visual signal, a kanban. This visual signal, in turn, tells the supermarket employee to stock the shelve.

- **The Failure Mode and Effects Analysis (FMEA)** is useful in the Improve stage because your activities include listing potential solutions, ranking them, selecting solutions, rolling out or implementing the solutions and evaluating them. In the FMEA the problem in a process is graphically mapped showing the key inputs and outputs of each process step. The effects of the potential failure modes are listed and then compared with each other to find weaknesses in the process and areas for improvement. They are scored and assigned categories of Severity, Occurrence and Detection. The higher the score, the more severe, the more frequent and the harder it is to detect the failure mode. Then, the risk priority numbers are calculated. A risk priority number (RPN) is found by multiplying each failure mode's Severity, Occurrence and Detection, giving a number from 1 to 100. After ranking the RPNs in descending order, the first areas to attack using the DMAIC approach are found. The bigger the number, the more important the failure mode is in improving the process

- **Queuing Theory** is a collection of mathematical models of various queuing systems. Queues have an input source, an arrival pattern, which can be static or dynamic, the control depends on the nature of arrival rate (random or constant). There are two aspects of a service system, the configuration of the service system, and the speed of the service. In a queuing system, the speed with which service is provided can be expressed in either of two ways as service rate and as service time.

Single Server – Single Queue - The models that involve one queue – one service station facility are called single server models where customer waits till the service point is ready to take them for servicing.

Single Server – Several Queues – In this type of facility there are several queues and the customer may join any one of these but there is only one service channel.

Several (Parallel) Servers – Single Queue - In this type of model there is more than one server and each server provides the same type of facility. The customers wait in a single queue until one of the service channels is ready to take them in for servicing.

Several Servers – Several Queues - This type of model consists of several servers where each of the servers has a different queue. Different cash counters in an electricity office where the customers can make payment of their electric bills is an example.

Service facilities in a series - In this type a customer enters the first station and gets a portion of service and then moves on to the next station, gets some service and then again moves on to the next station and finally leaves the system, having received the complete service.

- The **5S method** is a tool to control outcomes and make improvements to keep track of the changes implemented. It stands for sort, straighten, shine, standardize, and sustain. It can be used for any process or service. Sorting is just as it states, organizing and separating what you need and don't need.

Straighten means to straighten up and arrange items you need for your process or service so they are easily identified. Shine means to clean up your area and set it up where you can keep it clean. Standardize means to organize the first three s's so everything has a place. Sustain means to keep it going in all of your areas. The 5 S method improves safety and communication, improves process flow, increases compliance, reduces space requirements, boosts morale, removes non value added steps, and reduces wasted time looking for items.

- 5S helps by eliminating the unnecessary, establishing a place for what remains, and cleaning up remaining equipment, tools, and storage devices. This helps reduce clutter and needed items are readily found. Visual cues and visual management are used to improve consistency. These are signs, labels, stickers, and cards marking where things go.

Step	Japanese	Literal Translation	English
Step 1	*Seiri*	Clearing up	Sorting
Step 2	*Seiton*	Organizing	Straightening
Step 3	*Seiso*	Cleaning	Shining
Step 4	*Seketsu*	Standardizing	Standardizing
Step 5	*Shitsuke*	Training and discipline	Sustaining

- **Error-proofing** is also known as **Poka Yoke.** Poka Yoke is a concept in quality that means mistake proofing. The phrase initiated in Japan during the 1960s by Shigeo Shingo who was one of the industrial engineers at Toyota. The initial term was baka yoke, but a worker at Arakawa Body Company refused to use baka yoke mechanisms in her work area because baka yoke had a dishonorable and offensive connotation. Hence, the term was changed to poka yoke, which means mistake proofing. The process to apply poka yoke is:
  - Identify the operation or process based on a Pareto Chart.
  - Analyze the 5 whys and understand the ways a process can fail.
  - Decide the right poka yoke approach, such as using a shut out type or an attention type that an error has been made.

- A poka yoke can be electrical, mechanical, procedural, visual, human or any other form that prevents incorrect execution of a process step. Poka yoke helps people and processes work right the first time. Poka yoke builds in techniques that make it impossible to make mistakes. These techniques can drive defects out of products and processes and substantially improve quality and reliability. Poka-yoke can be used wherever something can go wrong or an error can be made.

- **Value-stream mapping** is a visual tool used to document the flow of products or services through a system. A value stream is all of the actions required to change raw materials into a product delivered to the customer. The map separates the value added activities of a system from the non-value added activities. The non-value-added activities are opportunities for possible improvement within the system. The Value stream shows the process flow from order to delivery.

1. **Value-added and non-value-added activities**
   a. **Identify waste in terms of excess inventory, space, test inspection, rework, transportation, storage, etc., and reduce cycle time to improve throughput.**

Value added activities are those which transform information or material into a product of value to the customer. Basically any activity that improves the activity is value added.

Non Value added activities are those which have negative return on the investment of resources and can typically be eliminated without impairing a process. Examples of these include:

- Waiting for materials to be brought to production
- Time spent searching for materials, tools, supplies, or information not in their proper location
- Multiple trips to get the right repair parts and tools
- Equipment failures causing idle time
- Bottlenecks that create dead time
- Waiting for approvals or direction from leadership

Here is a chart of the Six Sigma Tools and activities to use at each phase.

Six Sigma Greenbelt Tools		
DMAIC Phase	**Activities Involved**	**Tools You Can Use**
DEFINE *Define the problem, agree on the goals, and listen to the voice of the customer.*	Develop project name and purpose Complete project charter Develop a high-level process map Identify process owner, champion, team Define customers and requirements CTQ Align goals with business initiatives Determine projected ROI	Project charter template Brainstorming Graphs Stakeholder analysis Historical data Voice of the customer
MEASURE *What is your baseline?*	Collect data Take measurements Develop detailed process maps Measure your measurement system	Data collection plan Benchmarking CTQs, histogram, Pareto chart, scatter Diagram, control charts, Sigma level, ROI, FMEA, validate, gage R&R
ANALYZE *Analyze the data for variation and root causes.*	Analyze data Define performance objectives Identify value and non-value processes Determine the root cause	Value-stream, historical data 5 whys, fishbone, hypothesis testing, DOE, histogram, Pareto chart, scatter diagram, control charts, statistical analysis
IMPROVE *Choose the solution/s, pilot the solution, mistake proof, roll out the improvement, and evaluate the results*	List potential solutions Rank solutions Select solution and try Check results Roll out Evaluate improvement	Analysis, brainstorming Decision matrix Capability study Pilot Implementation plan
CONTROL	Verify improvement processes	Sigma, ROI, balance scorecard, control chart

Theory of constraints

The "Theory of Constraints" is the management philosophy of Eliyahu M. Goldratt. He introduced it in his 1984 book called *The Goal*. The overall premise is that a system can only produce as fast as the slowest step. The throughput of the system, therefore, can be improved with a focused effort to improve that step called the constraint. The theory of constraints uses five steps to improve performance:

- Identify the current constraint
- Exploit quick improvements to the throughput of the constraint using existing resources
- Subordinate and review all other activities in the process to ensure that they are aligned with and support the needs of the constraint
- Elevate if the constraint still exists to consider what further actions can be taken to eliminate it from being the constraint
- Repeat The Five Focusing Steps

1. **Design for Six Sigma (DFSS) in the organization**
   a. **Quality function deployment (QFD)**
   b. **Describe how QFD fits into the overall DFSS process.**

Quality function deployment initiated in 1966. It was a method for new product development under Total Quality Control initiatives. Dr. Shigeru Mizuno and Yoji Akao. Developed many of the methods of quality deployment in 1972. Then in 1978 the Japan Society of Quality Control formed a research group to specifically study Quality Function Deployment.

QFD is used to translate customer requirements to engineering specifications providing linkage customers, designers, competitors, and manufacturing. QFD incorporates the voice of the customer in the design of the product or service to better design and satisfy the customer's needs. It is best used early in the design phase using these four steps:

1. Product planning to translate customer requirement into the product technical requirements to meet them.

2. Product design transferring technical requirements to key product characteristics

3. Process planning to identify process operations necessary to achieve the characteristics in step 2.

4. Process Control to control operations.

Design for Six Sigma

Design for Six Sigma (DFSS) is different from DMAIC as it is used for designing a completely new product or process that meets customer specifications. DFSS vary from organization to organization depending on the characteristics of the product or business process that needs to be developed. DFSS is an approach based methodology rather than a standalone optimization methodology such as DMAIC. DMADV and IDOV are variations of the DSS.

1. **Design and process failure mode and effects analysis (DFMEA & PFMEA)**
2. **Define and distinguish between design FMEA (DFMEA) and process (PFMEA) and interpret associated data.**

Design FMEA uses the application of the Failure Mode and Effects Analysis method specifically to design a product to determine ways that a product design might fail in real-world use.

Process FMEA is a structured analytical tool used to identify and evaluate the potential failures of a process for existing products or services. The FMEA evaluates each process step and assigns a score on a scale of 1 to 10 for the following variables:

- **Severity** which assesses the impact of the failure mode with 1 representing the least safety concern and 10 representing the most dangerous safety concern.
- **Occurrence** which assesses the chance of a failure happening with 1 representing the lowest occurrence and 10 representing the highest occurrence.
- **Detection** which assesses the chance of a failure being detected with 1 representing the highest chance of detection and 10 representing the lowest chance of detection.
- **Risk priority** number which calculates the RPN= severity X occurrence X detection. Any RPN value exceeding 80 requires a corrective action.

1. **Road maps for DFSS**
2. **Describe and distinguish between DMADV (define, measure, analyze, design, verify) and IDOV (identify, design, optimize, verify), identify how they relate to DMAIC and how they help close the loop on improving the end product/process during the design (DFSS) phase.**

DMADV (define, measure, analyze, design, verify) The DMADV model is used for new products or services requiring design and product verification.

IDOV (identify, design, optimize, verify) is a popular methodology for designing products and services to meet six sigma standards. In the identify phase identification of customer needs is very essential for launching a new product or service and requires performing competitive analysis and identify critical-to-quality factors. The design phase determines functional requirements and available options. The Optimize Phase assesses the tolerance level of a business process to predict the performance capability of a business process and developing alternative design elements. The Validate Phase tests and validates the selected design.

Six Sigma – *Define* (25 Questions)

1. **Process Management for Projects Process elements**
   a. **Define and describe process components and boundaries.**
   b. **Recognize how processes cross various functional areas and the challenges that result for process improvement efforts.**

Process management for the project relies heavily on project management skills and following the project plan. The steps in the management of Six Sigma involves:

- Develop the project name and purpose
- Complete the project charter
- Develop a high level process map
- Identify the process owner, champion, and team
- Define the customers and requirements critical to quality
- Align goals with the business initiatives
- Determine the projected Return on Investment

The return on investment is a critical component of deciding whether or not to move forward with a project. The ROI is a measure of the overall effectiveness of a Six Sigma teams ability to produce the desired outcome. The formula for the project ROI is

$$ROI = \frac{Cost\ Savings}{Asset\ investment + Labor\ Cost + Miscellaneous\ Investment}$$

1. **Owners and stakeholders**
   a. **Identify process owners, internal and external customers, and other stakeholders in a project.**

In a Six Sigma project a **stakeholder** is anyone who is actively involved in the project and has interests that may be positively or negatively affected by the performance or completion of the project. They may exert influence over the project, its deliverables or its team members. Other stakeholders are:

- The management, who provides the strategic objectives and alignment.
- The project sponsor, who transfers project budget authority.
- The project manager, who coordinates the project and team members who implement the project plan and charter.

- The team, who is developed through the project charter and selection of the champion and executive management team.

Quite often a **customer** is the person or group who drives the project and is the focus of a project. Customers define requirements, needs or wants. They have a vested interest in a project. They also, pay for the project, support resource needs and evaluate and use the results of the project. They provide the "Voice of the Project" and are considered the "Voice of the Customer".

1. **Identify customers**

   a**. Identify and classify internal and external customers as applicable to a particular project, and show how projects impact customers.**

Internal customers are organizational division, sections, units or employees who are the receiver of products, materials, services or information from other units in the organization. This could be engineering, logistics, housekeeping, supervisors, purchasing etc.

External customers are customers who are not employed by the organization but are users or purchases of the products or services. This could be shippers, part suppliers, or buyers.

1. **Collect customer data**
   a. **Use various methods to collect customer feedback (e.g., surveys, focus groups, interviews, observation) and identify the key elements that make these tools effective.**
   b. **Review survey questions to eliminate bias, vagueness, etc.**

The collection of customer data through surveys, interviews, in person focus groups email or phone help the green belt to determine the needs of the customer and the voice of the customer. When sampling data a good sample is **representative of the population**. And each sample point represents the attributes of a known number of population elements. All probability sampling methods rely on random sampling. In survey research the measurement process includes the environment the survey is conducted in, the way that questions are asked, and the state or status of the survey respondent. A survey produces a sample statistic which is used to estimate a population parameter. The variability among statistics from different samples is called sampling error.

- **Bias** occurs when the survey sample does not accurately represent the population. The bias that results from an unrepresentative sample is called **selection bias**.
- **Under-coverage bias** occurs when some members of the population are inadequately represented in the sample.
  Nonresponse bias occurs when individuals chosen for the sample are unwilling or unable to participate in the survey.

> **Voluntary response bias** occurs when sample members are self-selected volunteers the resulting sample tends to over-represent individuals who have strong opinions.
>
> - **Random sampling** is a sampling from a population in which the selection of a sample unit is based on chance and every element of the population has a known, non-zero probability of being selected. Random sampling helps produce representative samples by eliminating voluntary response bias and guarding against under coverage bias.
> - **Response bias** is bias that results from problems in the measurement process. Bias due to measurement error can occur with a poor measurement process. This includes **leading questions** where the wording of the question may be loaded in some way to favor one response over another. **Social desirability** occurs when survey respondents are reluctant to admit to questions in the survey if the results are not confidential. Their responses may be biased toward what they believe is socially desirable.

1. **Analyze customer data**
   a. **Use graphical, statistical, and qualitative tools to analyze customer feedback.**

Customer survey and feedback data can be displayed by any of the tools in the Define, Measure, or Analyze phases to represent the current actual state of customer satisfaction and quality goals. The data display tools should be reflective of the positive and negative aspects of the data.

1. **Translate customer requirements**
   a. **Assist in translating customer feedback into project goals and objectives, including critical to quality (CTQ) attributes and requirements statements.**
   b. **Use voice of the customer analysis tools such as quality function deployment (QFD) to translate customer requirements into performance measures.**

The purpose of the Voice of the customer (VOC) survey is to identify key business drivers of internal and external customer satisfaction. The VOC is necessary to properly focus the project and develop the right measures. The VOC asks what each customer desires specifically what is important to them and what do they perceive is a defect in a quality or service. This is a template for the VOC survey (for a restaurant) and sources of information:

Voice of the Customer (VOC)

The questions were used to investigate what is important to the customers.

Who	What & Why
Customers and Stratification/Segmentation (Identify customer groups that may have different needs.)	The what and why Indicate specifically what you want to know about your customers. The customer survey was designed with these factors in mind.
Customers – What's important? Excellent food quality, value for money, quality service (speed) and atmosphere. A defect is a variance from these expectations.	
Kitchen staff - What's important? Provide high quality food which showcases chef and line cook expertise and cooking skills. A defect is a returned entrée, appetizer, or desert with inconsistent quality.	• What's important to you? • What's a defect? • How are we doing? How do we compare to our competitors? • What do you like? What don't you like? • What are your expectations?
Management - What's important? Be the restaurant of choice for customers. Maintain a repeat customer base. A defect is any failure point in service dimensions.	
Wait staff - What's important? Satisfied customers and consistent service resulting financial compensation. A defect is any factor which prohibits customers from vacating with less than satisfactory experience.	
Buss Staff - What's important? Satisfied wait staff and resulting financial compensation. A defect is the inability to maintain adequate supply of clean tables to satisfy customer demand.	
Host staff - What's important? Satisfied customers resulting financial compensation. A defect is the unavailability of tables for guests.	

Sources

REACTIVE SOURCES	PROACTIVE SOURCES
Complaints Web page activity Sales reporting	Interviews Surveys Comment cards Direct observation Market research/monitoring Benchmarking Quality scorecards

This is a survey for data collection.

Customer Satisfaction Survey Help us improve or "wait times"		
Were you given an estimated wait time?	Yes	No
Were you offered a choice of seating?		
Were you escorted to your table?		
Were you greeted in a reasonable amount of time?		
Was your appetizer served in a reasonable amount of time?		
Was your entree served in a reasonable amount of time?		
Was your dessert served in a reasonable amount of time?		
Was your table cleared as needed?		
Was your check presented in a timely manner		
Thank you for your patronage at Johnson Cafe and helping us improve our service to our valued customers.		

The survey helps the green belt to determine appropriate measures for time throughput, efficiency, and time.

1. **Project management basics**
   a. **Project charter and problem statement**
   b. **Define and describe elements of a project charter and develop a problem statement, including baseline and improvement goals.**

The project charter tells the project purpose, scope, deliverables, responsibilities, executive sponsor, project sponsor, roles, issue escalation procedures, implementation plans, milestones, major assumptions, and risks. The specific parts are as follows:

Project Scope, the project scope is to coordinate and conduct regular project team conference calls, identify and manage project milestones, and assign required resources at the appropriate stages of the project including:

- Deliverables
- Project Charter
- Communication and status reporting processes
- Applicable training
- Responsibilities
- Executive Sponsor

The Executive Sponsor will be primarily responsible and accountable to:

- Lead the Project Steering Committee as Chairperson

- Approve the vision, purpose and objectives of the project
- Ensure the project remains tightly aligned with the overall mission, vision and funding

Project Sponsor

The Project Sponsor will be primarily responsible and accountable to:

- Approve the requirements, timetables and resources
- Approve the provision of funds and resources
- Authorize acceptance of the final solutions delivered by the project

Project Manager

The Project Manager will be primarily responsible and accountable to:

- Deliver the project on time, within established fiscal parameters and to specification
- Manage and direct project staff, suppliers, and project stakeholders
- Undertake the activities required to initiate, plan, execute and close the project successfully.

Sample Project Charter		
Project Title/Number		
Reducing Surgical		
Site Infections	Revision: One	Date: June 12, 2012
Sponsoring Organization		
Houston Medical Center		
Date Chartered June 14, 2012	Project start date: June 20, 2012	Target completion date: August 31, 2012
Project Champion	Name: Scott Hardin, Chief of Staff Office Location: 332B	Phone: (404) 384 3832 Mailstop 10
Project Leader	Name: Elizabeth Strong Office Location: 408C	Phone: (404) 383 8723 Mailstop 92
Project Black Belt	Name: Kyle Evans Office Location: 516A	Phone: (404) 383 3998 Mailstop 114
Project Green Belt	Name: Glenna Graves Office Location: 112A	Phone: (404) 383 1704 Mailstop 106
Faculty Mentor (as applicable)	Name: Ryan Hart Office Location: 302B	Phone: (404) 383 1024 Mailstop 81

Sample Project Charter		
	Title/Role:	Phone:
	Anil Kuhn, Chief of Surgery	Phone: (404) 383 2657
	Ahmad Radi, Chief of Specialty Care	Phone: (404) 383 1119
Principle Stakeholders	Sara Scott, Executive Nurse	Phone: (404) 383 1123
	Shelly Meade, Ward Nurse	Phone: (404) 383 1678
	Joan Meany, Infection Control Nurse	Phone: (404) 383 8922
	John Roland, Chief Housekeeping	Phone: (404) 383 6255

1. **Project scope**
   a. **Assist with the development of project definition/scope using Pareto charts, process maps, etc.**

The green belt will develop or assist in the development of the project scope which includes which deliverables will be achieved through the project and which will not be included in the project.

1. **Project metrics**
   a. **Assist with the development of primary and consequential metrics (e.g., quality, cycle time, cost) and establish key project metrics that relate to the voice of the customer.**

The voice of the customer will determine what improvements are desired and need to be made. All improvements are done with the goal of increasing the quality of the business output. The three key input components of quality are the customer, the employee, and the process. The customers define the quality of a good or service and are the key decision makers. They expect reliability, competitive prices, great performance, and efficient delivery. Once you determine the customers' requirements you need to determine what data is needed to make improvements. There are several ways to display this data.

1. **Project planning tools**
   a. **Use project tools such as Gantt charts, critical path method (CPM), and program evaluation and review technique (PERT) charts, etc.**

Project planning is important for establishing your project's timeline with realistic and attainable deadlines. The plan and timeline will make sure that you spend appropriate amounts of time on each step of the process and help keep you on track. Typically Gantt, CPM or PERT charts are used to visually display tasks, deliverables, milestones, and resource constraints in a continuum which is called the critical path and is the minimum amount of time needed for the completion of the project.

1. **Project documentation**
   a. **Provide input and select the proper vehicle for presenting project documentation (e.g., spreadsheet output, storyboards, etc.) at phase reviews, management reviews and other presentations.**

Project documentation vehicles will vary with the organization but the information used to develop the presentations should be included in the project plan or project dashboard.

1. **Project risk analysis**
   a. **Describe the purpose and benefit of project risk analysis, including resources, financials, impact on customers and other stakeholders, etc.**

A project risk analysis helps determine the risk for the organization in relation to the benefits of the project. A risk breakdown structure is often used and it lists all potential risks identified as being possible, an estimate of the likelihood of occurrence, an outline of how to reduce the risk's likelihood, and strategies for minimizing the consequences. Risks typically fall under four categories.

- **Management** risks which are those factors resulting from shortages of resources, changing priorities or conflicts between the project and current procedures.
- **Implementation** Risks which occur when development of new techniques or processes is part of the project.
- **External** risks which result from changes outside of the organization such as government regulations, economic conditions, or competition.
- **Operational** risks are caused by the project itself such as being over budget or behind schedule.

1. **Project closure**
   a. **Describe the objectives achieved and apply the lessons learned to identify additional opportunities.**

The Project Closure Report is the final document produced for the project and is used by senior management to assess the success of the project, identify best practices for future projects, resolve all open issues, and formally close the project. The Project Closure Report is created to accomplish the following goals:

- Confirm outstanding issues, risks, and recommendations.
- Improve on project activities and team communication.
- Review and validate the milestones and success of the project.
- Outline tasks and activities required to close the project.
- Identify project highlights and best practices for future projects.
- Determine if the original goals were met.
- Determine project highlights and best practices.
- Ensure all of the project deliverables were met.

- Determine who will measure continuing progress
- Review post-project tasks
- Develop metrics for performance recommendations
- Training requirements

1. **Management and planning tools**
   a. **Define, select, and use 1) affinity diagrams, 2) interrelationship digraphs, 3) tree diagrams, 4) prioritization matrices, 5) matrix diagrams, 6) process decision program (PDPC) charts, and 7) activity network diagrams.**
   - **Affinity diagrams** are used when issues seem too large and complex to grasp and when group consensus is necessary. The affinity diagram organizes a large number of ideas into their natural relationships using team creativity and is often used during brainstorming
   - **Interrelationship digraphs are used to show** the relationship among factors in a complex situation. It shows the relationship of multiple factors in a map like diagram or relations diagram.
   - **Tree diagrams show** the hierarchy of tasks and subtasks needed to complete an objective. When the drawing is complete it resembles a tree. It is used to break down broad categories into finer and finer levels of detail. It aids in developing logical steps to achieve an objective
   - **Prioritization matrices** are tools to compare the alternative actions or choices when a clear choice is not easily understood or apparent through using brainstorming techniques, action planning and issue analysis then scoring the results.
   - **Matrix diagrams** are a planning tool for displaying the relationships among various data sets. During the Champion Phase or initial phase charter phase of the Define stage organizations often use a prioritization matrix to rank competing priorities. This is a scoring or ranking system it can also be a tool for the voice of the customer. If the customer has multiple issues requiring quality control they can rank them in order of priority to the organization. The sample shows the weighted section after weighted scoring on quality, efficiency and performance aspects. The following chart shows a weighted Six Sigma project prioritization matrix.

	Weightage	Ratings			Weighted Scores		
		Solution 1	Solution 2	Solution 3	Solution 1	Solution 2	Solution 3
High Accuracy and Precision	10	8	7	9	80	70	90
Promise to Delivery	9	6	7	8	54	63	72
Reliability	7	9	8	9	63	56	63
Cost	8	8	9	5	64	72	40
Program Management	7	5	4	6	35	28	42
Turnaround Time	5	4	4	6	20	20	30
				Total	316	309	337

Process decision program (PDPC) charts

Process decision program charts identify what may go wrong in a plan under development. Once possible issues are identified prevention controls and countermeasures can be developed to prevent the problems. PDPC charts are used in these situations:

- When the price of failure is high
- Before implementing a plan
- When the plan must be completed on schedule

The steps used to develop the PDPC chart include developing a tree diagram of the proposed plan, reviewing each task brainstorming of what could go wrong, reviewing all the potential problems , for each potential problem brainstorm possible countermeasures, then determine which to implement.

Activity network diagrams are planning diagrams sometimes called arrow diagrams, pert charts, or the critical path method used to show activities that are in parallel or in series for a project. It shows the most likely times for the completion of projects.

1. **Business results for projects**
   a. **Process performance**
   b. **Calculate process performance metrics such as defects per unit (DPU), rolled throughput yield (RTY), cost of poor quality (COPQ), defects per million opportunities (DPMO) sigma levels and process capability indices.**
   c. **Track process performance measures to drive project decisions.**

Defects per unit (DPU) a defect is a product's or service's nonfulfillment of an intended requirement or reasonable expectation for use. These may be in the form of "blemishes," "imperfections" and "nonconformity." These are items that do not meet the customers expectations.

Rolled throughput yield (RTY) is the probability that a product will pass through the entire production or service process without rework and defects.

Cost of poor quality (COPQ) the concept of quality costs or the cost of poor quality was first mentioned by Joseph Juran in the Quality Control Handbook published in 195. The cost of poor quality or "Cost of Quality" referred to the costs associated with providing poor quality product or service.

Juran advocated the measurement of costs on a periodic basis as a management control tool. Research shows that the costs of poor quality can range from 15%-40% of business costs (e.g., rework, returns or complaints, reduced service levels, lost revenue). Finding and correcting mistakes consumes a large portion resources but many organizations to not keep statistics on this. Effective quality management decreases production costs because the sooner an error is found and corrected the less costly it will be.

The cost of quality has four elements:

- External Failure Costs which are those associated with defects found after the customer receives the product or service such as customer complaints.
- Internal Failure Costs are those associated with defects found before the customer receives the product or service such as scrap or rework.
- Inspection (appraisal) Cost is a cost incurred to determine the degree of conformance to quality requirements such as inspection and testing.
- Prevention Cost are those incurred to prevent poor quality such as quality improvement teams.

Defects per million opportunities (DPMO) a defect is an event of nonconformance to specification. Defects are most often measured in defects per unit (DPU), defects per opportunity (DPO), defects per million opportunities or a level of Sigma. A unit with one or more defects is defective. A unit may have multiple defects based on the number of opportunities. Defects are caused by errors and are most commonly measured using a c-chart or u-chart. The example below shows the calculation of defective parts per million opportunities using pencil production as a sample. The defects, numbers of opportunities, and numbers of units produced are calculated to determine the DPMO.

Defective Parts Per Million Opportunities DPMO

Pencils	Diameter	Paint	Eraser	Lead	Length	Defective	Defects Per Pencil
Pencil 1						No	0
Pencil 2					X	Yes	1
Pencil 3						No	0
Pencil 4	X		X			Yes	2
Pencil 5	X	X	X	X		Yes	4
Pencil 6				X		Yes	1
Pencil 7		X			X	Yes	2
Pencil 8			X			Yes	1
Pencil 9				X		Yes	1
Pencil 10	X	X	X			Yes	3
							15

	D	O	U		U	X	O	Equals	TOP 50
	15	5	10		10		5		50

				DPU	Equals	15	/	50	Equals	0.3

D is the number of defects

O is the number of opportunities for a defect

U is the number of units

TOP is the total number of opportunities = U times O

DPMO equals DPO times 1,000,000

Using our table

D equals 15 total defects

O equals 5 opportunities or categories of defect types

U equals 10 pencils

TOP equals U times O equals 50 total opportunities

DPU equals D divided by TOP which equals 1.5 defects per unit or 15 total defects divided by 10 pencils.

DPO equals 0.30

DPMO equals 300,000

Out of a million opportunities, the long term performance of the process would create 300,000 defects.

Sigma levels

Sigma levels determine the rate of defects and are standardized measure of the error rate of a process, based on the DPMO estimate. The Sigma Level estimate is a long-term estimate of the process. Sigma is an industry standard estimate of process Sigma Levels developed by Motorola and adopted throughout business and industry. A chart of sigma levels is below.

Sigma Performance Levels – One to Six Sigma	
Sigma Level	Defects Per Million Opportunities (DPMO)
1	690,000
2	308,537
3	66,807
4	6,210
5	233
6	3.4

Process capability indices show the value of the tolerance specified for the characteristic divided by the process capability. Cpk, Cp, Pp, and Ppk are most commonly used and defined as follows.

- C_p= Process Capability. A simple and straightforward indicator of process capability.

- C_{pk}= Process Capability Index. Adjustment of C_p for the effect of non-centered distribution.

- P_p= Process Performance. A simple and straightforward indicator of process performance.

- P_{pk}= Process Performance Index. Adjustment of P_p for the effect of non-centered distribution.

The formulas to calculate each are below:
- Pp = (USL – LSL) / 6 * Std.dev
- Cpl = (Mean – LSL) / 3 *Std.dev
- Cpu = (USL – Mean) / 3 *Std.dev
- Cpk= Min (Cpl, Cpu)

C_p **and** C_{pk}, are an index which measures how close a process is running to its specification limits, relative to the natural variability of the process. C_{pk} measures how close you are to your target and how consistent you are to around your average performance. You must have a C_{pk} of 1.33 4 sigma or higher to satisfy most customers.

Pp and Ppk process performance indexes verify if the sample generated from the process is capable to meet Customer CTQs (requirements). It differs from Process Capability in that Process Performance only applies to a specific batch of material. Process Performance is only used when process control cannot be evaluated.

Track process performance measures to drive project decisions
1. **Failure mode and effects analysis (FMEA)**
   a. **Define and describe failure mode and effects analysis (FMEA). Describe the purpose and use of scale criteria and calculate the risk priority number (RPN).**

Failure Mode and Effects Analysis - FMEA is systematized technique which identifies and ranks the potential failure modes of a design or manufacturing process in order to prioritize improvement actions. FMEA provides information in quantifying weighted priorities, risks and contributing characteristics of a problem. FMEA acts as a way of identifying and preventing problems before they occur. Failure modes are the ways, or modes, in which something might fail. The failures are any errors or defects in the product or service which affect the customer. Factors are prioritized according to how serious they are and how often they occur. The FMEA gives you an analysis where you can take action to eliminate or reduce failures immediately based on how you prioritize them. Risk Priority Numbers are assigned and are the value assigned to the severity and occurrence of each potential failure on scale of 1 to 10 or low to high. By multiplying these 2 factors the risk priority RPN is determined by and equals severity times the occurrence.

1. **Team dynamics and performance**
   a. **Team stages and dynamics**
   b. **Define and describe the stages of team evolution, including forming, storming, norming, performing, adjourning, and recognition. Identify and help resolve negative dynamics such as overbearing, dominant, or reluctant participants, the unquestioned acceptance of opinions as facts, groupthink, feuding, floundering, the rush to accomplishment, attribution, discounts, plops, digressions, tangents, etc.**

The green belt will be responsible to monitor group dynamics and resolve issues hindering performance. In general team development goes through four stages. Forming, Storming, Norming, and Performing.

- The forming state of a project team is marked by uncertainty and tentativeness there may be anticipation by some team members. Team members are getting used to each other.
- The storming stage begins as the team members become more comfortable and begin to express their differences in opinion.

- In the norming the team rallies around their ability to meet the team objective. They communicate well and trust one another.
- At the performing stage team members begin to see tangible results and have a high level of interaction.

1. **Six sigma and other team roles and responsibilities**
   a. **Describe and define the roles and responsibilities of participants on six sigma and other teams, including black belt, master black belt, green belt, champion, executive, coach, facilitator, team member, sponsor, process owner, etc.**

Roles & responsibilities, your organizations core team will vary with the size of your organization but the key players are identified on your project charter and will typically look like this:

- The champion is responsible for program oversight, project selection, project evaluation, and project advocacy.
- Project leadership is provided by the six sigma black belt or green belt they provide team mentorship.
- The project team is responsible for data collection, data analysis, and the implementation strategy.

In a six sigma project a stakeholder is anyone who is actively involved in the project and has interests that may be positively or negatively affected by the performance or completion of the project. They may exert influence over the project, its deliverables or its team members.

Quite often a customer is the person or group who drives the project and is the focus of a project. Customers define requirements, needs or wants. They have a vested interest in a project. They also, pay for the project, support resource needs and evaluate and use the results of the project. They provide the "Voice of the Project" and are considered the "voice of the customer".

Other stakeholders are:

- The management, who provides the strategic objectives and alignment.
- The project sponsor, who transfers project budget authority.
- The project manager, who coordinates the project and team members who implement the project plan and charter.
- The team, who is developed through the project charter and selection of the champion and executive management team.
- A Yellow Belt has a basic knowledge of Six Sigma but does not lead project teams.
- A Green Belt is a person trained in the six sigma methodology who is a team member of six sigma process improvement action teams.
- A Black Belt is a person who is part of the leadership structure for process improvement teams.

- A Master Black Belt is a person trained in the six sigma methodology who acts as the organizational Six Sigma director or a program manager.

Six Sigma Team Roles

1. **Team tools**
   a. **Define and apply team tools such as brainstorming, nominal group technique, multi-voting, etc.**

A green belt will use team tools to engage project team members through communication and collaboration. Using brainstorming, mind mapping or nominal group techniques allows team members to create, modify, and develop projects collectively on a common problem. Typical questions include: What they are doing on a project? What are the deliverables? What information do they need? What is the end result?

A team facilitator will keep the discussion progressing forward with relevant conversation to advance the project while monitoring behavior or team members to prevent negative project outcome.

1. **Communication**
   a. **Use effective and appropriate communication techniques for different situations to overcome barriers to project success.**

Team communication is crucial to project performance. The team and facilitator or green belt should determine the best forms of communication to progressively advance the project. What works best, frequent face to face interaction, conference calls, or emails? Many times this will depend on the duration and complexity of a project as well as the stakeholder level of involvement. A stakeholder analysis may be required based on potential impact on the project and perceived attitudes and/or risks.

Some common roadblocks to quality improvement include:
- Conflict among team members
- Knowledge which is not available

- Communication
- Motivation
- Change
- Lack of Creative Thinking
- Lack of Critical Thinking
- Lack of Project Management

Project teams are composed of diverse groups of people. Each team differs in composition and each team will function differently depending on the leadership style of the team leader. It is important to recognize cultural differences and team conflict. It is crucial to have constant communication and information flow. Team members will need to be developed and guided through the Six Sigma project through performance feedback.

The project manager is responsible for initiating the team or teams. They build the business case and facilitate initiating the process. The project team provides research, analysis and support. The stakeholders provide input and processes which define the scope.

Team members are brought together through the **project team charter**. They are identified for the role in the process or expertise to improve the quality.

It is important that team members first understand their goals. They must understand the ground rules of the team such as punctuality, respect, responsibilities, and etiquette. Attendance is critical almost mandatory.

As you set up a team make sure you provide a list of the objectives and an agenda for each meeting to keep on task. Use active listening skills while communicating at the team meetings and encourage the teamwork mentality. Make sure you provide support and consistent follow up on open items. This is the best time to ask questions.

Maslow's hierarchy of needs is a model of human perception of needs. Maslow was a clinical psychologist who observed a predictable sequence of perceived needs that individuals attempt to satisfy. After the basic needs are met individuals work to satisfy the next need in the hierarchy.

These five needs form a pyramid beginning with physiological needs which are the basic needs of food, shelter, and clothing. The next layer of the pyramid is safety needs which are the absence of threat to a person, family or finances. The mid level of the pyramid is the social need to interrelate and socialize with others. The fourth level is the esteem level which shows the human need for recognition, acknowledgement and respect of peers and community. The top of the pyramid is self actualization which is the need for ultimate individual human potential to be satisfied or fulfilled.

Maslow's hierarchy explains how individuals focus on their needs first then on the needs of the project group. This is human nature. Knowing that people will often take care of themselves first will go a long way as you manage teams.

Conflict in a six sigma project can be common and inevitable. Conflict is incompatible objectives and perceptions driven by individual or team goals which are not aligned with the project goals.

In order to manage conflict it is best to be proactive by being prepared, acknowledging conflict, and managing it. By being prepared as a project manager you understand that you should expect conflict on teams. The level and source of conflict an be projected. A project manager should acknowledge conflict by confronting it proactively addressing concerns and issues. Finally, project managers should manage the conflict response. This can be done by force. Using force, project managers assert force because deadlines are constraining a project. Project managers can avoid an issue when it is of little significance and no major impact on a project. They can be accommodating when the issue is of great importance of a team member and impacting it will increase your goodwill with the team. You can collaborate when goals overlap and compromise when equal power parties have incompatible goals.

Good leadership requires being able to select the appropriate leadership style. The leadership style should reflect the variables of a project such as the development stage of your team forming, storming, norming, performing; the phase of the project, and environmental factors.

In project management there are four leadership styles for team approach.

- **Delegating** is useful for teams which are empowered and self directing. This democratic style, draws on people's knowledge and skills, and creates a group commitment to the resulting goals
- **Supporting** leadership style is used for teams that require continual support in terms of competencies and experience. Emphasizes the importance of team work and creates harmony.
- **Coaching** is used for those teams on the verge of being self directed. It focuses on developing individuals, showing them how to improve their performance, and helping to connect to the goals of the organization.
- **Directing** leadership is used for teams which are new or on time sensitive projects. The commanding style is classic model of "military" style leadership – probably the most often used, but the least often effective.

Because it rarely involves praise and frequently employs criticism and it undercuts morale and job satisfaction.

Six Sigma – *Measure* (30 Questions)

The purpose of the Measure Phase is to give a true and accurate picture of the current condition as it relates to the project. The measure phase determines exactly what will be analyzed in the analysis phase. During this phase the green belt will perform the following:

- Select the characteristics in processes that are Critical to Quality
- Define what that process outputs should be
- Define the defect for the process
- Determine the inputs to the process that contribute to defects
- Define the ROI for eliminating defects in terms of increased profitability or cost savings
- Measure the defects that affect CTQ's
- Perform a Measurement Systems Analysis to ensure defects are properly measured

Activities involved are in the measure phase include collecting data, taking measurements, developing process maps, and developing a measuring system.

Tools used during the measuring phase include a data collection plan, benchmarking, CTQs, histogram, pareto chart, scatter diagram, control charts, sigma level, ROI, FMEA, and Gauge R&R.

In the measure phase the green belt will determine what to measure, review processes and systems to determine key steps in the process, determine the tools to use such as process flow charts, determine how to gather data, and develop the data collection plan.

The data collection plan houses information relative the process or service which needs to be measured to improve. This includes the parameters such as the conditions to be measured, definitions, and collection methods. Following is a chart with data collection information and a sample for an assembly line.

Data Collection Plan

	Define What to Measure			Define How to Measure			Who will Do it?	Sample Plan			
Measure	Type of Measure	Operational Definition	Measurement or Test Method	Data Tags Needed to Stratify the Data	Data Collection Method	Person(s) Assigned	What?	Where?	When?	How Many?
Name of parameter or condition to be measured	X or Y attribute or discrete data, product or process data	Clear definition of the measurement defined in such a way as to achieve repeatable results from multiple observers	Visual inspection or automated test? Test instruments are defined. Procedures for data collection are defined.	Data tags are defined for the measure. Such as: time, date, location, tester, line, customer, buyer, operator, etc.	Manual? Spreadsheet? Computer based? etc.	State who has the responsibility?	What measure is being collected	Location for data collection	How often the data is collected	The number of data points collected per sample

Data Collection Plan

Metric	Who will collect Data?	Operational Definition	Sample Size/	Data Type (Continuous, discrete)	Source/location	Collection method	How will data be used?	How will data be displayed?
Percentage of Downtime	Kevin Reilly	Amount of time the assembly line is stopped in a 12 hour shift.	20 Minute Increments	Continuous throughout the shift	Line timer 7	Manual Print	Monthly Trending	Histogram

1. **Process modeling**
   a. **Develop and review process maps, written procedures, work instructions, flowcharts, etc.**

The green belt will develop project related documents including process maps, written procedures, work instructions and visual aids to document project actions and improvement activities. Process modeling is an analytical representation or illustration of an organization's business processes. Modeling allows you to consider changes in a system, current or planned, under different situations to optimize the outcome. Models can be simple mathematical models, but more complex models can provide a more realistic picture of the system you are studying. This example shows process costing so an organization is able to determine the flow of costs.

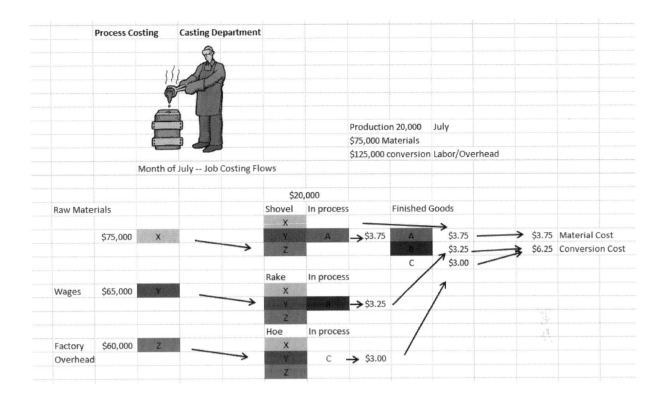

This example shows a value stream map where peanut butter and jelly sandwiches are made and packaged. It shows the time between each phase and the total time for processing as well as total amount per day.

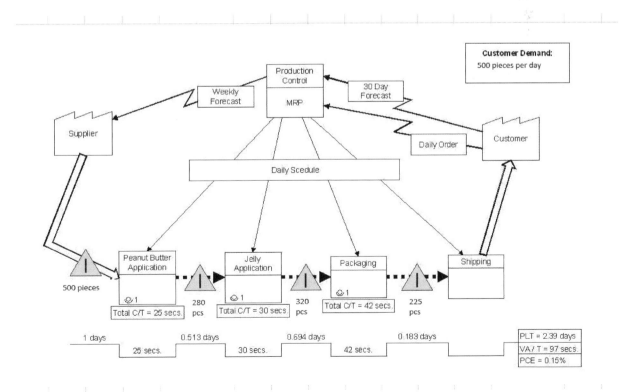

1. **Process inputs and outputs**
   a. **Identify process input variables and process output variables (SIPOC), and document their relationships through cause and effect diagrams, relational matrices, etc.**

The SIPOC diagram identifies key input and output variables for processes. SIPOC stands for suppliers, Inputs, Process, Outputs, and Customers.

SIPOC

	Who are the suppliers for our product or service?	What do the suppliers provide to my process?		What are the start and end points of the process associated with the problem and the major steps in the process.		What product or service does the process deliver to the customer?		Who are the customers for our product or service? What are their requirements for performance

Suppliers		Input		Process (High Level)		Output		Customers	
1	Psychiatrist	1		**Start Point:**			Behavior management	1	Patients with
		2		Build a referral mechanism	1		Education	2	diagnosis of:
		3	Clinical Referral				Reduced costs	1	Depression/Anxiety
2	Psychologists	1					Improved care	2	Patients with
		2		**Operation or Activity**	2		Improved productivity	1	diagnosis of: Bipolar
		3	Clinical Referral	1	Survey providers		Improved efficiency	2	Mood Disorder
3	Social Workers/	1		2	Meet with providers		Patient empowerment	1	Patients with
	transition team	2		3	Educate	3	Patient satisfaction	2	diagnosis of: Post
		3	Clinical Referral	4	Build referral efficiency		Effective use of resources	1	Traumatic Stress
4	Nurses	1	Clinical Referral	5	Build a wait list		Patient focus	2	Patients with
		2	Chart Review	6		4		1	diagnosis of:
		3		7				2	Schizophrenia
5	Physician Assistants	1		8				2	Patients with
		2		9		5		1	diagnosis of:
		3	Clinical Referral	10				2	Substance abuse
6	Other mental health	1		11				2	Patients with
	providers	2		12		6		1	diagnosis of:
		3	Clinical Referral	13				2	Dementia Caregiver
7	Patient groups self	1		14				2	Medical Center
	referral	2		15		7		1	Reduced costs
		3	Self Referral	16				2	
				17					
				End Point:					
				Control, monitor, and share					

The current state process map shows the options or steps as a process is at the present state prior to changes.

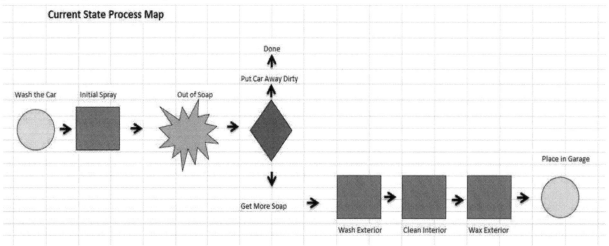

1. **Probability and statistics**
   a. **Drawing valid statistical conclusions**
   b. **Distinguish between enumerative (descriptive) and analytical (inferential) studies, and distinguish between a population parameter and a sample statistic.**

Enumerative and **analytic** statistical studies provide a rational basis for action to improve quality. Enumerative studies take action on the subject or data being studied and is a statistical study on the results of the studied material. Analytic studies take action on the process or system cause that produces the subject or data being studied and focuses on improving the system that created the results. Both have the goal of improving the process or service. Deming introduced both studies in the book *Some Theory of Sampling*. A statistical study can be enumerative or analytic, but it cannot be both. Deming stated management should be analytic instead of enumerative continually focusing on future results not past results.

Population parameter and a sample statistic

A **population parameter** is a number describing something about a whole population such as the population mean or mode. It is fixed and used as the value of a variable in a general distribution. The population parameter is used in statistics and is a measurement of the population that is being studied large populations are often measured by taking samples to represent the entire population.

A **sample statistic** is something that describes a sample such as the sample mean. In statistics a sample statistic is one that is a subset of individuals from within a statistical population to estimate characteristics of the whole population.

1. **Central limit theorem and sampling distribution of the mean**
   a. **Define the central limit theorem and describe its significance in the application of inferential statistics for confidence intervals, control charts, etc.**

The **central limit theorem** explains why many distributions tend to be close to the normal distribution. The central limit theorem describes the characteristics of the population of the means created from the means of an infinite number of random population samples of size.

The central limit theorem predicts that:

- The distribution of means will increasingly approximate a normal distribution as the size N of samples increases.
- The standard deviation of the population of means is always equal to the standard deviation of the parent population divided by the square root of the sample size (N).
- The mean of the population of means is always equal to the mean of the parent population from which the population samples were drawn.

1. **Basic probability concepts**
   Describe and apply concepts such as independence, mutually exclusive, multiplication rules, etc.

Independent probability occurs if the occurrence of one of the events provides no information about whether or not the other event will occur meaning the events have no influence on each other.

Mutually Exclusive probability is a statistical term used to describe a situation where the occurrence of one event is not influenced or caused by another event.

Multiplication

Conditional probability is the probability of an event given the information that an event B has occurred indicated by P(A/B).

Order of operators is important when simplifying expressions and equations. The order of operations is a standard that defines the order in which operations such as addition, subtraction, multiplication and division occur. The Order of Operations is shown below. The acronym PEMDAS is often used.

- **Parentheses and brackets** includes simplifying the inside of parentheses and brackets before the set of parentheses or remove the parentheses.
- **Exponents** includes simplifying the exponent of a number or of a set of parentheses before you multiply, divide, add, or subtract it.
- **Multiplication and Division** includes simplifying multiplication and division in the order that they appear from left to right.
- **Addition and Subtraction** includes simplifying addition and subtraction in the order that they appear from left to right.

1. **Collecting and summarizing data**

Types of data and measurement scales
Identify and classify continuous (variables) and discrete (attributes) data. Describe and define nominal, ordinal, interval, and ratio measurement scales. (Analyze)

Continuous variables can have an infinite number of different values between two given points an example of this is employees, you could have 10, 20, or 30 but not 10.1, 20.5, or 30.4.

Discrete data is data that cannot be broken down into a smaller units. Only a finite number of values are possible. Discrete data has one of a set of discrete values such as pass or fail or yes or no.

Six Sigma projects use several techniques to evaluate data and compare it to quality standards. Data collection and analysis allows for quality assurance as a project progresses to assure the project satisfies the required quality standards. Some of the more common quality control techniques which easily represent to stakeholders and Six Sigma project managers whether a project is doing well or not are:

- **Pareto Diagrams** which help ensure a balance between effort and resources. The Pareto principle states that 20 percent of inputs result in 80 percent of outputs.
- **Trend analyses** can show if the improvements implemented in your project are improving from the baseline or benchmarks.
- **Histograms** are used to show improvements over time.
- **Scatter diagrams** are also used and they show the correlations between variables.

How measurements are examined at both the key process output variable KPOV and key process input variable KPIV levels is important. The four measurement data scales are **nominal, ordinal, interval, and ratio**. It is important to understand what your measurements are and what their ranges can be. **Nominal** data examines whether data are equivalent to a particular value such counts of coins you have pennies for 1 cent, nickels for five cents, dimes for 10 cents, and quarters for 25 cents. **Ordinal** data has ordering but value differences are not important. An example of this is employee satisfaction on the Likert scale ranking of 1 to 5 where 5 is satisfied and 1 is dissatisfied. Ordinal data can be ranked but the differences between ordinal values cannot be quantified. **Interval** data has ordering with a constant scale but no natural zero. An example of this is temperature. There is no difference between the two measures of say 38 degrees and 43 degrees or 75 degrees and 80 degrees. There is still a five degree difference. **Ratio** scale is ordered with a constant scale and has a natural zero examples of this are height, age, weight, and length. You can say that a 10 lb turkey weighs twice as much as a 20 lb turkey.

Continuous variables are numeric values that can be ordered sequentially and do not fall into discrete ranges. Examples are weight and time. If a variable can take on any value between two specified values, it is called a continuous variable; otherwise, it is called a discrete variable.

1. **Data collection methods**
   a. **Define and apply methods for collecting data such as check sheets, coded data, etc.**

The green belt will collect data and store it in checksheets or any storage document use by the organization i.e checklist, spreadsheet, coded form, computer generated list etc. This is a fabricated sample data collection plan for a car company which shows the type of data and how it will be collected.

Data Collection Plan Jane's Car Company

Metric or Measure	Who will collect Data?	Operational Definition	Sample Size/Frequency	Data Type Unit	Source/location	Collection method	How will data be used?	How will data be displayed?
Assembly Line Stop	John Smith	Number of times the assembly line stops	Per 8 Hour Shift	Minutes	Assembly Line Timer Unit 7	Automated Paper Tape	Averaged over Seven Days	Histogram Chart
Proper Bolt Alignment	Scott Johnson	Number of Fender Set Stops	Per 24 Hour Shift	Minutes	Fender Bender Machine Set	Automated Paper Tape	Averaged over Seven Days	Histogram by Day of Week

1. **Techniques for assuring data accuracy and integrity**
    a. **Define and apply techniques such as random sampling, stratified sampling, sample homogeneity, etc.**

Random sampling helps to achieve unbiased sample results in a study by choosing subjects from a population through unpredictable means. All of the subjects have an equal chance of being selected out of the population being researched. Three methods are commonly used for random sampling include random number tables, mathematical algorithms, and physical randomization devices.

Stratified sampling is used to ensure smaller sub-groups are not overlooked. Stratified sampling is used when there are smaller sub-groups that need to be investigated, when you want to reduce standard error, and when you want to achieve greater statistical significance in a smaller sample.

Sample homogeneity means the characteristics of the sample are uniform and representative of the population.

1. **Descriptive statistics**
    a. **Define, compute, and interpret measures of dispersion and central tendency, and construct and interpret frequency distributions and cumulative frequency distributions.**

Central tendency shows the locality or centrality of the data. The most common measures are the average, mean, median and mode.

Frequency distributions

The pattern of variation in a set of data is called a distribution. A distribution can be described using the terms shape, center, and spread.

- Shape: Is the distribution symmetric?
- Center: What is the most common value for the variable?
- Spread: How much variation is present?

A **histogram** is a graphing technique used to display a distribution.

1. **Graphical methods**
   a. **Depict relationships by constructing, applying and interpreting diagrams and charts such as stem-and-leaf plots, box-and-whisker plots, run charts, scatter diagrams, Pareto charts, etc.**
   b. **Depict distributions by constructing, applying and interpreting diagrams such as histograms, normal probability plots, etc.**

Any data analysis should consist of the following: Histogram, Trend Graph and/or Pareto Graph if applicable, an estimate of the center and spread of the data, a description of the sampling plan, how many measurements and how they were collected, measurement units, and other relevant information with accompanying explanations to the diagrams and data.

Data analysis asks these questions:

- Is the distribution stable?
- Does this variable change over time?
- Are there other factors that influence the behavior of this variable?
- What is the relationship of this variable with other variables?

The green belt will use numerous tools to depict data relationships. The most common tools with an example follow:

This chart shows a trend analysis. A trend analysis shows data over an extended timeframe to determine if quality or production is improving or worsening. In this example the actual sales are greater than the projected sales after quarter1. The chart shows the numerical data and a graphic chart.

Trend Analysis			Automobile Sales	
	Quarter 1	Quarter 2	Quarter 3	Quarter 4
Projected Sales	758	444	560	719
Actual Sales	567	771	638	818

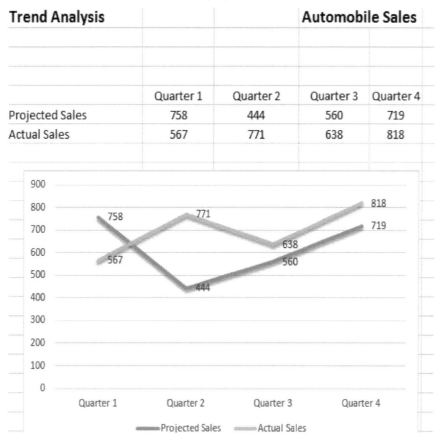

This sample histogram shows in chart form for textbook sales. This provides a visualization for a project that sales have decreased from August through November.

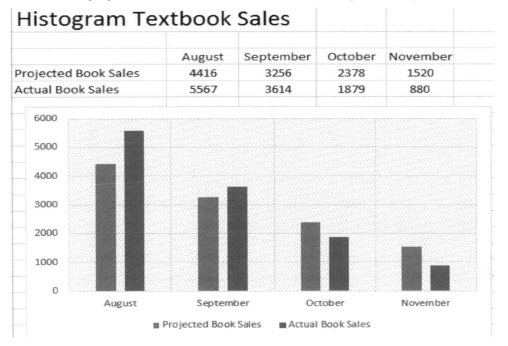

Histogram Textbook Sales

	August	September	October	November
Projected Book Sales	4416	3256	2378	1520
Actual Book Sales	5567	3614	1879	880

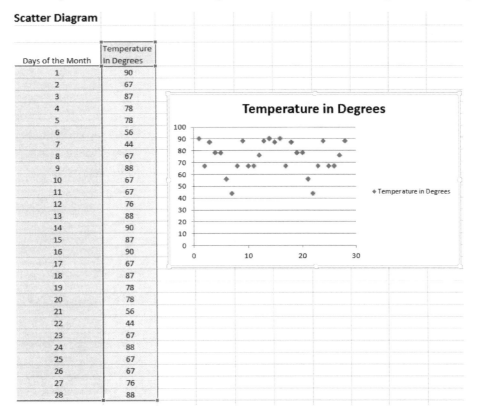

This sample scatter diagram provides a visualization for a project takes the ambient variable temperature for a month and places them in a scatter diagram for analysis.

Scatter Diagram

Days of the Month	Temperature in Degrees
1	90
2	67
3	87
4	78
5	78
6	56
7	44
8	67
9	88
10	67
11	67
12	76
13	88
14	90
15	87
16	90
17	67
18	87
19	78
20	78
21	56
22	44
23	67
24	88
25	67
26	67
27	76
28	88

This is a sample of a process map showing the operators for decision points in a simple process such as leaving home in the morning for work. Notice the quality actions for activities which add value or check for defects.

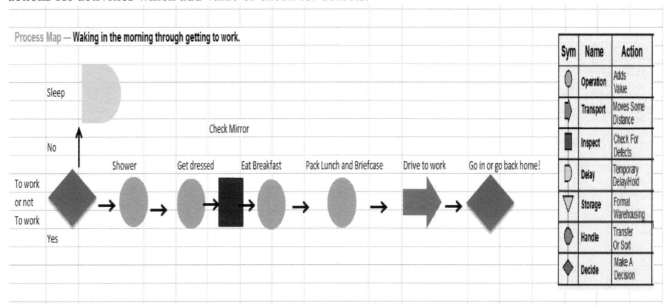

Pareto Chart Favorite Foods

Food Type	Favorite
Pizza	1
Spaghetti	1
Salad	1
Hamburgers	1
Chicken	1
Wraps	1
Hamburgers	1
Chicken	1
Wraps	1
Pizza	1
Spaghetti	1
Salad	1
Hamburgers	1
Chicken	1
Wraps	1
Pizza	1
Spaghetti	1
Salad	1
Hamburgers	1
Chicken	1
Pizza	1
Spaghetti	1
Salad	1
Hamburgers	1
Chicken	1
Wraps	1

Food Type	Total
Chicken	9
Hamburgers	8
Pizza	5
Salad	15
Spaghetti	6
Wraps	6

This is a sample of a Pareto chart which takes a sample of favorite foods then calculates the sum of each subset and the total. The same principle can be used for any green belt data set.

Favorite food types

■ Chicken ■ Hamburgers ■ Pizza ■ Salad ■ Spaghetti ■ Wraps

Box Plots are used to represent relatively small data sets. The outliers are points that are more than 1.5 times the interquartile range above the third quartile or below the first quartile. The whiskers extend to the largest and smallest data values that are not outliers.

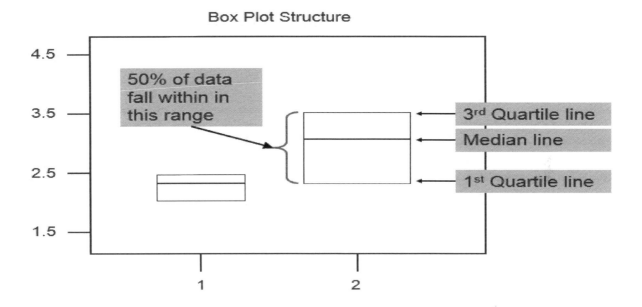

1. **Probability distributions**
   a. **Describe and interpret normal, binomial, and Poisson, chi square, Student's t, and F distributions.**

Normal distribution is a continuous distribution where any two data values may have an interval in between. The bell shaped normal curve has probabilities that are found as the area between any two z values. Normal distribution has 5 characteristics:

- The mean, mode, and median are equal
- Most values concentrate near the mean and decrease in frequency further from the mean
- Symmetrical about the central value
- The curve has only one mode
- All data points fall within the curve either 50% to the left or 50% to the right

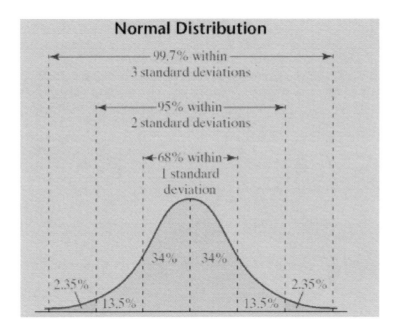

Binomial distribution is different from a normal distribution although the shape of the curve will be similar. The binomial distribution is a discrete probability distribution. It shows the probability of getting "X" successes in a sample of "N" from an 'infinite' population where the probability of a success is "Y'".

Poisson distribution is a discrete probability distribution. It is used when the sample size is not restricted and it is not possible to specify the number of occurrences but you do know the average number of occurrences: The formula is shown here where d = the number of occurrences and λ =the average number of occurrences.

$$P(d) = \frac{\lambda^{d} e^{-\lambda}}{d!}$$

Chi square is used to test whether a sample is drawn from a population that conforms to a specified distribution. chi square is also called goodness of fit. chi square is calculated by summing the chi square contributions from each category in the hypothesis. The hypothesis is:

H0 the sample conforms to the specified distribution

H1 the sample does not conform to the distribution

The formula for calculating chi square is shown here where Ai = the actual value for category 'i' and Ei = the expected value for category   'i'

$$\chi^{2} = \sum_{i=1}^{3} \frac{(A_{i} - E_{i})^{2}}{E_{i}}$$

Student's t is a Probability Distribution Function which gives the height of the distribution. The shape of the t distribution is similar to the normal distribution, and converges on the normal distribution as the number of degrees of freedom increases:

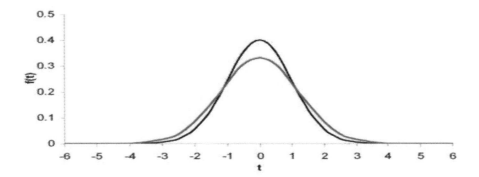

F distributions are a continuous probability distribution formed from the ratios of two chi-squared variables. If X1 and X2 are independent chi-square variables. The formula for calculation is shown here:

$$F = \frac{X_1 / \upsilon_1}{X_2 / \upsilon_2}$$

- **T-test** compare the mean against a specified value using a sample of 30 items or less
- **Two sample t-test** compare the means of two samples of 30 items less
- **Paired t-test** comparing the means of two samples of 30 items or less, when the items in the two samples can be paired
- **Z-test** compare the mean against a specified value when the sample has more than 30 items or the standard deviation is known

1. **Measurement system analysis**
   a. **Calculate, analyze, and interpret measurement system capability using repeatability and reproducibility (GR&R), measurement correlation, bias, linearity, percent agreement, and precision/tolerance (P/T).**

The Gage Repeatability and Reproducibility is the amount of measurement variation introduced by a measurement system, which consists of the measuring instrument itself and the individuals using the instrument. Depending on the source you may see Gauge R&R or Gage R&R spellings. A Gage R&R study quantifies three things:

- Repeatability – variation from the measurement instrument
- Reproducibility – variation from the individuals using the instrument
- Overall Gage R&R, which is the combined effect of (1) and (2)

The Repeatability and reproducibility (GR&R) sample below shows this process is at 17% which is in the marginal range.

	Value	% of Tolerance	
Repeatability: Equipment Variation (EV)	1.039	12%	Reducing Measurement System Variation
Reproducibility: Appraiser Variation (AV)	1.183	13%	
Overall GR&R:	1.574	17%	(as a rule, 10% or less is acceptable, 10% to 20% is marginal, over 20% is unacceptable)

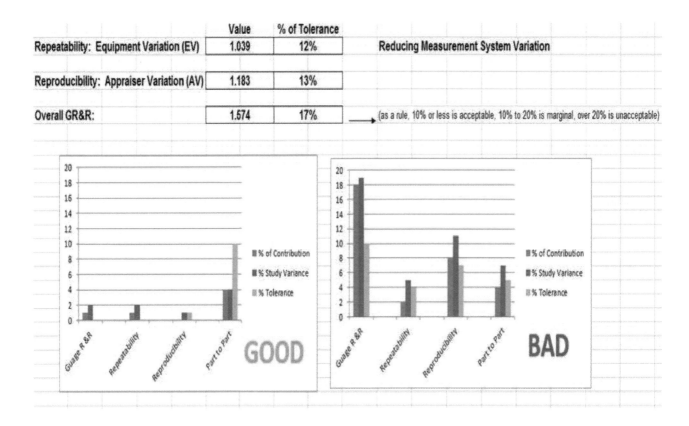

- **Measurement correlation** measures the strength of a linear relationship between two variables.
- **Bias Measurement** occurs when information collected for use as a study variable is inaccurate.
- **Linearity** is the variation between a known standard across the low and high end of a gauge. It is the difference between an individual measurements and the known standard.
- **Percent agreement** is used in a Measurement Systems Analysis and is the percentage of the total number of units inspected where there is agreement. It can be used to compare one appraiser or tester to another.
- **Variability** is the measure of the dispersion of a data set and includes these measures: range, standard deviation, standard error, variance, and coefficient of variation.
- **Precision/tolerance (P/T)** tells how well a given measurement can be reproduced. This is a standard deviation around a mean value. Tolerance may have two errors systematic and random.
- **Accuracy** is how close a measured value is to the true value. To determine the accuracy of a measurement requires calibration of the analytical method with known standard.

1. **Process capability and performance**
   a. **Process capability studies**
      Identify, describe, and apply the elements of designing and

conducting process capability studies, including identifying characteristics, identifying specifications and tolerances, developing sampling plans, and verifying stability and normality.

Process Capability Studies are short-term studies conducted to collect information on the performance of new or revised processes related to customer requirements. This occurs when processes, employees, or equipment change and as many possible measurements should be used to get an accurate reflection. Process capability examines the variability in process characteristics and whether the process is capable of producing products which conform to the required specifications. These are the formulas to calculate process capability:

- Cp = (USL-LSL)/6s
- Cpu = (USL-Xbar)/3s
- Cpl = (Xbar-LSL)/3s
- Cpk = Minimum of (Cpu,Cpl)

1. **Process performance vs. specification**
   a. **Distinguish between natural process limits and specification limits, and calculate process performance metrics such as percent defective.**

Natural process limits measure variation in a process. The natural process limits are positioned at plus and minus three standard deviations from the target. Thus, if the process is stable, about 99.7% of the process output will be within the natural process limits.

Specification limits are limits required by the customer which the supplier must ensure the process can produce to the required process capability value or specification.

Process capability indices
Define, select, and calculate C_p and C_{pk}, and assess process capability. The calculation to compute Cpk is:

$$C_{pk} = \text{minimum} \left\{ \frac{USL - \mu}{3\hat{\sigma}_R}, \frac{\mu - LSL}{3\hat{\sigma}_R} \right\}$$

Process performance indices
Define, select, and calculate P_p, P_{pk}, C_{pm}, and assess process performance. The calculation to compute Ppk is:

$$P_p = \frac{USL - LSL}{6\hat{\sigma}_{RMSE}}$$

1. **Short-term vs. long-term capability**
   a. **Describe the assumptions and conventions that are appropriate when only short-term data are collected and when only attributes data are available.**
   b. **Describe the changes in relationships that occur when long-term data are used, and interpret the relationship between long- and short-term capabilities as it relates to a 1.5 sigma shift.**

Long-term capability are the process performance indices Pp and Ppk process capability measures. This is because the standard deviation used in their calculation is calculated using the Root Mean Square Error method which is inflated by shifts in the process mean.

Short-term capability are the process performance indices Cp and Cpk process capability measures. The standard deviation used in their calculation is calculated using the Range Method which is not affected by changes to the process mean.

1. **Process capability for attributes data**
   a. **Compute the sigma level for a process and describe its relationship to P_{pk}.**

The Sigma level is calculated using the normal distributionit is not usually practical to set the processes mean exactly on target and the mean of most processes is subject to drift right or left so a 1.5 standard deviation offset is assumed in converting between DPMO and Sigma Level.

Six Sigma – *Analyze* (15 Questions)

The analysis phase looks at data for variation and root causes. Activities involved in the analysis phase are: analyze data, define performance objectives, identify value and non-value processes and determine the root cause.

Tools you can use are:

- Process Maps
- Takt Time
- Data Sampling - Population vs. Sample
- Data Classification
- Data Collection
- SPC-Charts to assess Measurement System Stability
- MSA - Measurement System Analysis
- Statistical Process Control (SPC) Charts
- Root Cause Analysis
- 5-WHY
- Fishbone Diagram / Ishakawa Diagram / Cause and Effect Diagram
- Correlation Matrix
- FMEA - Failure Mode Effects and Analysis
- Overall Equipment Effectiveness (OEE)
- Spaghetti Diagram
- Establishing a Baseline Measurement
- DPU - Defects per Unit
- DPO - Defects per Opportunity
- DPMO - Defects per Million Opportunities
- Process Yield Metrics
- FY - Final Yield
- TPY - Throughput Yield

1. **Exploratory data analysis**

Multi-vari studies

Create and interpret multi-vari studies to interpret the difference between positional, cyclical, and temporal variation; apply sampling plans to investigate the largest sources of variation.

1. **Simple linear correlation and regression**
   a. **Interpret the correlation coefficient and determine its statistical significance (p-value); recognize the difference between correlation and causation.**
   b. **Interpret the linear regression equation and determine its statistical significance (p-value).**
   c. **Use regression models for estimation and prediction.**

1. **Hypothesis testing basics**
   a. **Define and distinguish between statistical and practical significance and apply tests for significance level, power, type I and type II errors.**
   b. **Determine appropriate sample size for various test.**

The significance level is the the probability of making a Type I Error. In a Hypothesis Test a Type I error occurs when statistically unlikely test results lead to the incorrect conclusion that the null hypothesis should be rejected.

1. **Single-factor analysis of variance (ANOVA)**
    a. **Define terms related to one-way ANOVAs and interpret their results and data plots.**

Analysis of Variance (ANOVA) is a statistical technique for analyzing experimental data. It subdivides the total variation of a data set into meaningful component parts associated with specific sources of variation in order to test a hypothesis on the parameters of the model or to estimate variance components. ANOVA is used to test whether the means of many samples differ but it does so using variation instead of mean. It compares the amount of variation within the samples to the amount of variation between the means of samples. ANOVA is effective to separate inherent variance and special cause variance and it also provides a methodology to evaluate the robustness of a process to various levels of a factor .

1. **Chi square**
    a. **Define and interpret chi square and use it to determine statistical significance.**

Chi square is used to test whether a sample drawn from a population conforms to a specified distribution. The formula to compute is:

$$\chi^2 = \sum_{i=1}^{3} \frac{(A_i - E_i)^2}{E_i}$$

Six Sigma – *Improve & Control* (15 Questions)

The improve phase chooses solutions, pilots the solution, performs mistake proofing, roll out the improvement and evaluate the results. Activities involved are to list potential solutions, rank solutions, select solutions to trial, check results, roll out and evaluate improvement.

Tools you can use are Analysis, Brainstorming, Decision Matrix, Capability Study, Pilot, and Implementation Plan

Control phase Activities involved include verify the voice of the customer is being met, check ROI, implement control plan and close out the project, verify improvement processes, document procedures, update standard operating procedures and policies, build a transition plan, and close Out the Project

Tools you can use are Sigma, ROI, Balance Scorecard, Control Chart, Control Plan Document, Control Plan Form, Transition Plan and Project Management Methods for Closing.

1. **Design of experiments (DOE)**
    a. **Basic terms**

    b. **Define and describe basic DOE terms such as independent and dependent variables, factors and levels, response, treatment, error, repetition, and replication.**

Design of Experiments is used when a process is affected by several different factors. In an experimental design several factors are varied at the same time. Experimental design involves conducting a systematic series of tests to discover the relationship between the factors that affect a process and the response. Instead of evaluating single factors multiple factors are evaluated and interactions between factors are evaluated and the effects of interactions between factors. Common DOE are the Taguchi methods Factorial Designs and Fractional Factorial Designs.

1. **Statistical process control (SPC)**
2. **Objectives and benefits**
    a. **Describe the objectives and benefits of SPC, including controlling process performance, identifying special and common causes, etc.**
3. **Selection and application of control charts**
    a. **Identify, select, construct, and apply control charts**

Control charts are used to monitor the output of a process. They are used to give timely warning of 'special causes' entering the process. They generally monitor either the process mean, the process variation or a combination of both. This picture depicts a control chart showing the range of data for an operation.

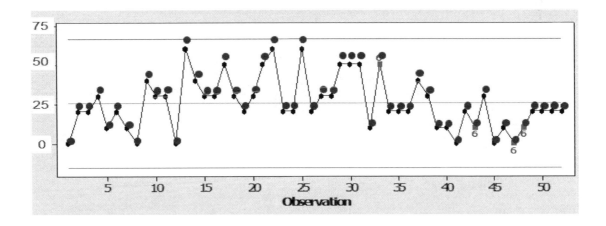

p Control Charts attribute charts used to plot units nonconforming when the samples are not of equal size. The formula to calculate p control charts is:

Upper Control Limit

$$UCL_p = \bar{p} + 3\sqrt{\frac{\bar{p}(1-\bar{p})}{n}}$$

Lower Control Limit

$$LCL_p = \bar{p} - 3\sqrt{\frac{\bar{p}(1-\bar{p})}{n}}$$

np Control Charts are attribute charts used to plot units nonconforming when samples of equal size are taken from the process.

Upper Control Limit

$$LCL_{np} = n\bar{p} - 3\sqrt{n\bar{p}(1-\bar{p})}$$

Lower Control Limit

$$UCL_{np} = n\bar{p} + 3\sqrt{n\bar{p}(1-\bar{p})}$$

c Control Charts are a control chart used to plot the number of nonconformities per unit when the sample size is constant. It is used in situations where each unit can have several nonconformities.

Upper Control Limit

$$UCL_c = \bar{c} + 3\sqrt{\bar{c}}$$

Lower Control Limit

$$LCL_c = \bar{c} - 3\sqrt{\bar{c}}$$

u Control Charts are used to plot the number of nonconformities per unit when the sample size varies.

Analysis of control charts
1. **Interpret control charts and distinguish between common and special causes using rules for determining statistical control.**

A stable process is in statistical control and shows variation due to common causes and it produces predictable results consistently

An unstable process is out of statistical control and shows variation due to special cause. An unstable out of control condition can be a point, set of points or trend in data. Sigma levels 1, 2 and 3 are used to determine unstable conditions.

Control plan
1. Assist in developing a control plan to document and hold the gains, and assist in implementing controls and monitoring systems.

The most common way to keep your project in control is to use a control plan. A control plan is a document that lists what is monitored in a product, service, or process as far as characteristics of quality. The control plan plays an important part in sustaining product quality long after a manufacturing process is developed and launched. There is no set type or style of project control plan for a specified particular improvement. Use a combination of spreadsheets and text documents to keep track of the measures being improved. In general you determine all of the headers and labels for your control plan which are critical to quality, proven to be important to the customer, and including a hierarchical reference number.

Following is a sample control plan showing the characteristics to be evaluated, using what measurements, and what the final stability processes will be.

CONTROL PLAN													Revision Number	1.0	
													Date		
		Organization:													
		Location:													
Critical to Quality Characteristic	Sig. Char. #	Significant Characteristic Description	Chart Type	Chart Champion	Chart Location	Measurement Method	Measurement Study	Reaction Plan	Guage Number	Sampling Plan	Process Stability	Cp/Cpk
A	A-1											
	A-2											
B	B-1											
	B-2											

Test tips and final words

Depending on the certification provider you choose the **Measure** and **Analyze** phases of the DMAIC model typically compose approximately 50 percent or greater of the written test. So focus on these areas if in doubt of where to place your study time. Focus your time on the areas you feel you need the most study. You are the best judge of your learning style, personality, and time management. Ideally do not distribute your time equally per section. Focus on the areas you have experience in first then those where you may be guessing. There will be general quality and historical questions and some project management questions, after that you can basically be assured everything you are asked falls under one of five areas - Define, Measure, Analyze, Improve, and Control.

Many of the skills necessary for the Six Sigma Green Belt can be transferred from knowledge and experiences you have encountered or experienced in the day to day operations of your job such as charting, data population and spreadsheet development. The skills you learn by completing a project or through online training when adequately reviewed should be sufficient to help you pass the Six Sigma Green Belt Certification examination.

- Historical statistics say the passing rate of the SSGB is 67% but as high as 90% for some certification organizations. Those are good odds.
- Use caution with the questions containing always, never, except, not, most, and least. There's nothing worse than missing a question simply because you misread it.
- Skip the questions which have overly technical terms and return later to avoid time drain on your overall test.
- Make a checklist of topics that are concerning you as you near test time. Some of the questions will be mathematical in nature. Ensure you have not made simple mathematical errors.
- You already have the content outline, focus on your gaps in theoretical knowledge.
- Choose the answers that have words you know.
- Sometimes new information in the answer response not included in the original question is many times an incorrect answer.
- Be cautious sometimes the answers that "sound" correct are incorrect based on the structure of the sentences by the test writer. Some of the answers are set for failure based on wording alone.

1. The purpose of the Define phase of the six sigma methodology is to reach agreement on the scope and performance goals of a project. The deliverables of the Define phase include all of the following EXCEPT?
a. A data collection plan
b. A completed project charter
c. A high level process map
d. Completed project plans

2. A SIPOC map will help identify all of the following EXCEPT?
a. Process
b. Suppliers
c. Inputs
d. Observations

3. Which of the following flowchart and value stream symbols represents a decision point?
a.
b.
c.
d.

4. Financial criteria are often used by executive management and project champions to determine whether to undergo a project in terms of costs of the project and benefits to the organization. This is commonly called the?
a. Return on investment (ROI)
b. Project activation point (PAP)
c. Value analysis
d. Project cost modeling

5. The voice of the customer will determine what improvements are desired and need to be made. All improvements are done with the goal of increasing the quality of the business output. The three key input components of quality are listed below which one of the choices below is incorrect?
a. The customer
b. The employee
c. The value stream
d. The process

6. The _____ principle states that 20 percent of inputs result in 80 percent of outputs.
a. Taguchi
b. Pareto
c. Deming
d. Juran

7. Which process improvement diagram, picture, or chart would a greenbelt use to show if the improvements implemented in a project are improving from the baseline or benchmarks?
a. Pareto diagrams
b. Scatter diagrams
c. Histograms
d. Trend analyses

8. The scatter diagram graphs pairs of numerical data with one variable on each axis to look for a relationship between them. If the variables are correlated, the points will fall along a line or curve. The better the correlation, the tighter the points will be to the correlation line. Which of the following is NOT an application for a scatter diagram?
a. When you are trying to identify potential root causes of problems
b. When you know two variables are related
c. When you have paired numerical data
d. When your dependent variable may have multiple values for each value of your independent variable

9. In Quality ERA 3 quality assurance and good manufacturing practices are instituted. In this step products are designed, quality is built into the manufacturing steps. The manufacture is controlled, tested, and rejects discarded. The result is fewer product rejects due to manufacturing. Which timeframe was quality ERA 3?
a. 1950's to 1960's
b. 1920's to 1930's
c. 2000 to present
d. 1980 to 1990

10. The sigma symbol represents standard deviations from the normal range in a business process. The more deviation, the less desirable a product is. A Six Sigma business process is a process in which defective parts per million opportunities (DPMO) are determined and refined. Which level of sigma results in 66,807 defective parts per million?
a. 2nd Sigma level
b. 6th Sigma level
c. 3rd Sigma level
d. 4th Sigma level

11. Eli Whitney developed _____ in 1798 for use in mass production. This invention greatly increased production and quality.
a. The cotton gin
b. Interchangeable parts
c. A quality system
d. Steel forge ranking system

12. Which stage of team development is represented by team members becoming more comfortable and beginning to express their differences in opinion?
a. Forming
b. Storming
c. Norming
d. Performing

13. Which of the following responsibilities or duties would be aligned with those of a six sigma green belt?
a. Executing the actual work of the project through guidance provided from six sigma green belts and six sigma black belts
b. Responsible for sponsoring the project and allowing for commitment of organization resources to the six sigma project
c. Responsible for providing guidance and coaching others in the organization about the six sigma philosophy.
d. Perform the operations required for the six sigma project and work with the project team ensuring that appropriate deliverables are met.

14. The measure of central tendency where half the values are greater than or equal to it and half are less than or equal to it is?
a. The mean
b. The mode
c. The median
d. The average

15. Which measurement data scale would include measures such as height ages, weight, or length?
a. Nominal
b. Ordinal
c. Interval
d. Ratio

16. A Measurement System Analysis (MSA) is a designed experiment that seeks to identify the components of variation in the measurement. A Measurement Systems Analysis evaluates the test method, measuring instruments, and the entire process of obtaining measurements to ensure the integrity of data. Which of the following is NOT considered in a Measurement Systems Analysis?
a. Selecting the correct measurement and approach
b. Assessing procedures & operators
c. Determine the design of experiments
d. Assessing the measuring device

17. Which of the following descriptions of process capability is NOT correct?
a. Process Capability is a simple and straightforward indicator of process capability.
b. The more relaxed and wider the distribution the higher the Process Capability.
c. Process Capability is a process index that numerically describes variation relative to the tolerance or specifications.
d. Process Capability is a short term process index that numerically describes the within subgroup or potential capability of a process assuming it was analyzed and stays in control.

18. The cost of poor quality is measured differently depending on the industry. The first goal is to have all the cost of quality in the Appraisal and Prevention areas and zero Costs of Poor Quality. Which of the following is NOT an example of an external cost?
a. Complaints
b. Environmental costs
c. Warranties
d. Delivery

19. In correlation analysis the strength and direction of a correlation are defined and measured by its correlation coefficient (r). Values for correlation include all of the following EXCEPT?
a. 0 indicates absolute correlation
b. 0 indicates no correlation
c. −1 indicates a perfect negative correlation
d. 1 indicates a perfect positive correlation

20. Critical to quality (CTQs) are the internal critical quality parameters developed around what the customer wants and needs. Three of the following are process parameters that affect CTQ measures. Which one is NOT a process parameter that affects CTQ measures?
a. Internal procedural disagreement in measuring and monitoring tools.
b. The timing ratio computed by dividing the time remaining until due date by the work time remaining.
c. Noise caused by internal environments as a result of neighboring subsystems such as part to part or piece to piece variation.
d. Controllable parameters which deal with a product feature or process step that must be controlled to guarantee delivery of what the customer wants.

21. A confidence interval is a range around a measurement that conveys how precise the measurement is. The confidence interval impacts the level of confidence and is affected by the sample size, percentages, and population size. Using the statistical definition of the 95 percent confidence interval, if a poll of 100 people were taken _____.

a. 5 percent of respondents would be within the calculated confidence intervals and ninety five percent would be either higher or lower than the range of the confidence intervals.

b. 95 percent of respondents would be within the calculated confidence intervals and only one percent would be higher than the range of the confidence intervals.

c. 95 percent of respondents would be within the calculated confidence intervals and five percent would be either higher or lower than the range of the confidence intervals.

d. 95 percent of respondents would be within the calculated confidence intervals and ten percent would be lower than the range of the confidence intervals.

22. Failure Mode and Effects Analysis FMEAs are a systematic way of identifying and preventing problems before they occur and a proactive performance improvement tool to assist in new service design or existing processes. Failure modes determine the ways, or modes, in which something might fail. The effects analysis part of an FMEA studies what?

a. The improvement tools to be used

b. Which effects are included

c. Which mode fails

d. The consequences of the failures

23. Poka Yoke is a concept in quality that means mistake proofing and can eliminate operator errors, measurement errors or supplier errors. Which of the following processes is NOT an example of Poka Yoke application?

a. Developing a standard operating procedure for painters on an assembly line

b. Preventing setup errors such as using the wrong tooling or setting machine adjustments incorrectly

c. Advancing the speed of a frozen dinner assembly line

d. Prohibiting wrong parts used in the process

24. Which of the following is NOT correct related to hypothesis acceptance?

a. If the p Value is less than the alpha risk, reject the null hypothesis and accept the alternative hypothesis.

b. If the p Value is greater than the alpha risk, reject the null hypothesis and accept the alternative hypothesis.

c. If the p Value is less than alpha risk, fail to reject the Null hypothesis.

d. A sample size can be determined

25. If a CEO were asking why printing costs are costing so much for a company and as the greenbelt you had reviewed paper costs, electricity costs, internal delivery costs, equipment rental costs, employee production costs which would be the most effective means of validating information?
a. Using the project charter
b. Using control charts and process charts
c. Using the 5S method
d. Using a customer satisfaction survey

26. Special cause variation is found through process analysis, control charts or process documentation. Special cause variation is variability or variation that triggers an essential change that is needed. Which of the following may cause special cause variation?
a. You adequately foresee common cause variation
b. You don't identify an important variable
c. Natural variation is understood
d. Common cause variation is eliminated

27. There are many DPMO charts available to quantify defects analytically. If there are 4,261 defects per million opportunities, then the sigma level would be?
a. Closest to 2 sigma
b. Closest to 3 sigma
c. Closest to 4 sigma
d. Closest to 5 sigma

28. The project plan template is a warehouse of information on how to improve the process. It outlines pilot studies and small scale tests of proposed solutions. The project charter does all of the following EXCEPT?
a. Justifies the project efforts with financial impact
b. Defines roles of team members
c. Describes the problem and scope
d. Lists the tools to be used for the DMAIC

29. Prototyping is the process of building a working model called a prototype to test various aspects of a design, change or incorporate new ideas or improvements and react quickly to customer feedback at the improved product before implementing it on a large scale. What is the main function of prototyping?
a. Determine project costs
b. Determine customer needs
c. Reduces project risk and cost.
d. Determine needed quality tests

30. Walter Shewhart developed control charts in 1929 understanding variation had significant impact on quality. Which control chart is used to plot the mean and standard deviation of a subgroup more than 5?
a. U chart
b. X bar-s chart
c. X bar-R chart
d. X-R chart

31. In which application would a Spearman Rank Correlation coefficient be used?
a. A measure that determines equality of sample medians
b. A measure that calculates r and allows the user to calculate partial correlation coefficient
c. A measure that requires both variables be measured on an ordinal scale
d. A measure that determines the degree of association among classifications of ranked scores

32. In an FMEA the risk priority number is calculated by multiplying what?
a. Severity, Occurrence, and Detection
b. Risk, Opportunity, Options
c. Severity, Opportunity, Occurrence
d. Causation, Determination, Prevention

33. The analysis tool used to quantify the relationship between causes and effects would be?
a. FMEA
b. Multi variant analysis
c. Cause and effect analysis
d. Regression analysis

34. This formula denotes which process performance measure?

$$\frac{\text{Upper Specification Limit- Lower Specification Limit}}{6 \times \text{Process Standard Deviation}}$$

a. Cp
b. CPU
c. CPL
d. Cpk

35. Considering confidence intervals, which of the following is correct?
a. The width of the confidence interval increases as the population sample size increases.
b. A 90% confidence level will be wider than a 95% confidence interval.
c. The width of the confidence interval will increase as the population size decreases.
d. The width of the confidence interval decreases as the sample size increases.

36. A process flow chart would BEST be used for?
a. Prioritizing solutions
b. Determining the cause of delays in a process
c. Comparison of two variables
d. Determining an error rate

37. The percentage of a product that completes processing on an assembly line without any additional work, repair, or re-handling is the _____?
a. Work in process
b. Demand variation
c. First pass yield
d. Sigma capability

38. In lean six sigma the type of waste which is unevenness in work and demand flow would be?
a. Mura
b. Muri
c. Muda
d. Mask

39. Which of the following would NOT be considered a process metric?
a. Customer satisfaction
b. Sigma Level or DPMO
c. Speed or lead times
d. Equipment cost

40. In the measure and control stages which type of distribution would be used to estimate the number of instances of a condition occurring in a process or population?
a. Poisson distribution
b. Exponential distribution
c. Binomial distribution
d. Pearson distribution

41. Statistical distributions can be characterized by all of the following parameters EXCEPT?
a. Skewness
b. Kurtosis
c. Congruency
d. Central tendency

42. The correlation diagram below can show whether a cause and effect are related. The diagram shows what?

a. A positive correlation

b. A weak correlation

c. No correlation

d. A negative correlation

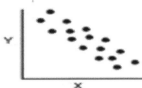

43. Scatter plots and scatter diagrams are used to investigate the possible relationship between two variables that both relate to the same event. If the points cluster in a band running from lower left to upper right, there is a positive correlation if ?

a. x decreases, y increases

b. x increases, y increases

c. x decreases, y decreases

d. x increases, y increases

44. The analysis which shows if the measurement system is equally accurate for large and small measurements and provides an indication of whether the bias error of a measurement system is constant throughout the range of equipment is?

a. Interpretation

b. Linearity analysis

c. Level loading

d. Standardization

45. Multi-vari plots are used to assign variation to all of the following EXCEPT?

a. Piece to piece variation

b. Within piece or sample variation

c. Time to time variation

d. Total variation

46. Which component of measurement error is the capacity of a system to produce the same values over time on measurement of the same sample?

a. Linearity

b. Stability

c. Accuracy

d. Bias

47. A PERT analysis determines probabilistic estimates of a cycle time or Project Schedule completion. The formula for PERT estimation is based on the central limit theorem and the variance is the standard deviation squared. Which of the following times is NOT included in the calculation?

a. Total cycle time

b. Pessimistic time

c. Optimistic time

d. Most likely time

48. Once a process capability index is calculated it can be converted to the corresponding sigma level. What does the process capability index show with a single number?
a. Estimated costs of production
b. Process critical path
c. Probability of errors
d. If the process can meet the requirements of a customer

49. The six sigma tool pictured here that determines customer desires and what quality attributes the customer requires and groups the requirements that are critical in requirement by function, schedule, and performance is the?
a. Customer solutions matrix
b. House of requirements
c. House of quality
d. Normal probability plot

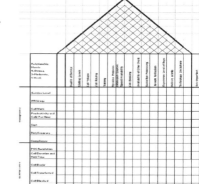

50. Simple linear regression is used when y is continuous and a single x variable exists. All of the following conditions also must be met EXCEPT?
a. The residuals have constant variance across all values of x
b. x can be ordinal or continuous
c. The residuals must be negative
d. The residuals are normally distributed

51. Compute the Mode, Mean, and Median of 5, 3, 23, 12, 8, 14, 29, and 24
a. Mode= none, Mean=14.75 Median=14
b. Mode= 12, Mean=14 Median=13
c. Mode= 5, Mean=10 Median=13
d. Mode= 8, Mean=12 Median=14

52. When comparing data conclusions about whether a process variation is consistent or is unpredictable can be determined by using these two formulas. They are used to calculate what?
a. Probability at 3 sigma and 1 sigma
b. Upper and lower control limits
c. Stem and leaf calculations
d. Static ratios

$$UCL_p = \overline{p} + 3\sqrt{\frac{\overline{p}(1-\overline{p})}{n}}$$

$$LCL_p = \overline{p} - 3\sqrt{\frac{\overline{p}(1-\overline{p})}{n}}$$

53. Which of the following is NOT an indication of an out-of-control signal in a control chart using a sample of approximately 20?
a. A run of four in a row are on the same side of the centerline.
b. Two out of three successive points are on the same side of the centerline and farther than 2 σ from it.
c. Four out of five successive points are on the same side of the centerline and farther than 1 σ from it
d. A single point outside the control limits

54. Variation is a change in data, characteristic, or function caused by one of four factors. Which of the following is NOT one of the four factors causing variation?
a. Special causes
b. Tampering
c. Common causes
d. Social variation

55. Deming wanted to transform management and offered _____ key principles to management for transforming business effectiveness.
a. Eleven
b. Twelve
c. Three
d. Fourteen

56. The method for keeping a process within boundaries or the act of minimizing the variation of a process is called the?
a. Process control
b. Process capability
c. Process capability index
d. Probability

57. Which set of International Standards Organization (ISO) standards covers quality management and quality assurance?
a. ISO 9001
b. ISO 1400
c. ISO 6000
d. ISO 1423

58. Which of the following elements is NOT included in the cost of quality or the costs associated with providing poor quality product or service?
a. External Failure Cost
b. Internal Failure Cost
c. Recycle Cost
d. Inspection (appraisal) Cost

59. Deming's theories and his System of Profound Knowledge consisted of four interrelated parts? Which of the following is NOT included?
a. Theory of Optimization
b. Theory of Analysis
c. Theory of Knowledge
d. Theory of Psychology

60. The DMAIC model is a data driven quality strategy for improving processes in the Six Sigma methodology. DMADV is a Six Sigma quality initiative for designing products and processes. What are the steps in the DMADV model?
a. Determine, measure, analyze, design and verify
b. Define, measure, act, design and verify
c. Describe, measure, actualize, determine, and verify
d. Define, measure, analyze, design and verify

61. Taiichi Ohno studied wastes and its impact on quality under his teachings there are how many forms of waste?
a. Four
b. Six
c. Seven
d. Eight

62. A quality metric that asks a question such as how many billing errors occurred in the last billing cycle is an example of what type of data?
a. Continuous
b. Binomial
c. Discrete
d. Congruent

63. A dataset positive correlation would have all of the following implications EXCEPT?
a. The independent variable decreases as the dependent variable increases.
b. The dependent variable increases as the independent variable increases.
c. The dependent variable decreases as the independent variable increases.
d. The dependent variable improves as the independent variable increases.

64. A dataset negative correlation would have all of the following implications EXCEPT?
a. The dependent variable decreases as the independent variable increases.
b. The dependent variable increases as the independent variable increases.
c. The independent variable decreases as the dependent variable decreases.
d. The dependent variable improves as the independent variable decreases.

65. The Pareto principle defined by J. M. Juran states that most effects come from relatively few causes. It shows _____ of the effects come from _____ of the possible causes.
a. All, a sample proportion
b. 10%, 90%
c. 20%, 80%
d. 80%, 20%

66. A quality tool used for collecting and analyzing data on the frequency or patterns of events, problems, defects, defect location, defect causes, particularly in production processes is the?
a. Check sheet
b. Scatter diagram
c. Control chart
d. Histogram

67. The six sigma tool used to improve a teams creativity and thinking, developed by Jiro Kawakita, which organizes a large number of ideas into their natural relationships is the?
a. Matrix diagram
b. Cause-and-effect/Ishikawa/fishbone diagram
c. Box and whisker plot
d. Affinity diagram

68. Which phase of the DMAIC model includes determining where problems or defects occur?
a. Define
b. Measure
c. Analyze
d. Improve

69. A green belt is determining the return on investment (ROI) for a project to measure the overall effectiveness of a Six Sigma project. ROI is calculated as

$$\text{ROI} = \frac{\text{Cost Savings}}{\text{Asset investment} + \text{Labor Cost} + \text{Miscellaneous Investment}}$$

Given a cost savings of $624,584, investment of $228,330 and labor of $42,638 calculate the ROI.
a. 2.30
b. 2.26
c. 1.98
d. 1.86

70. When working with probability theory, an expression or string of symbols intended to represent a numerical value must follow commonly accepted and unambiguous rules called the what?
a. Complimentary probability
b. Independent
c. Mutually exclusive
d. Order of operators

71. Which of the following is NOT a step in testing a hypothesis?
a. Determine benchmarks
b. State the Alternative Hypothesis Ha
c. State the Null Hypothesis Ho
d. Create Sampling Plan

72. A chart in which the critical work elements of a project are illustrated to portray their relationships to each other and to the project as a whole allowing the project manager predict outcomes based on various scenarios and ensuring optimum decisions are made about whether or not to adopt suggested procedures or changes is the what?
a. Gantt chart
b. Work breakdown structure
c. Pert chart
d. Alarm chart

73. A closed loop analysis accomplishes all of the following EXCEPT?
a. Determine business goals
b. Assess effectiveness
c. Continuous improvement
d. Aligns resources

74. The balanced scorecard is a strategic management system used to drive performance and accountability throughout the organization. All of the following are benefits of the balanced scorecard EXCEPT?
a. Alignment of individual and corporate objectives
b. Ethical balance is created
c. Culture driven by performance
d. Support of shareholder value creation

75. Which of the following reasons for the tests for means and variance is NOT correct?
a. Analysis of variance explains independence or norms
b. Fixed-effects models assume that the data came from normal populations which may differ only in their means
c. Means display the total combined effects of the data
d. Random effects models assume that the data describe a hierarchy of different populations whose differences are constrained by the hierarchy

76. Goldratt developed the Theory of Constraints that organizations can be measured and controlled by variations on three measures which include all of the following EXCEPT?
a. Employee motivation
b. Throughput
c. Operating expense
d. Inventory

77. Which of the following is a Japanese management philosophy used to increase time between failure (MTBF) or life of machinery?
a. TOC
b. VOC
c. CTR
d. TPM

78. Simple linear regression is used when y is continuous and a single x variable exists. The following conditions must also be met EXCEPT?
a. The residuals are normally distributed
b. X can be ordinal or continuous
c. The residuals have constant variance across all values of x
d. The residuals are dependent

79. Which of the following represents the number of defects divided by the number of products?
a. QFD
b. DPU
c. DPMO
d. COPQ

80. Which of the following is NOT a tool used in determining the project scope?
a. Product analysis
b. Data collection plan
c. Alternatives identification
d. Stakeholder analysis

81. A type of bar chart that illustrates a project schedule with start and finish dates of the terminal elements and summary elements of a project including the work breakdown structure and the dependency of relationships between activities would be the?
a. DFSS chart
b. House of quality
c. PERT chart
d. Gantt chart

82. A data analysis technique for determining if a measurement process has gone out of statistical control and is sensitive to changes in the number of defective items in the measurement process would be the?
a. Np chart
b. U chart
c. P chart
d. C chart

83. If it is impossible for two events to occur together these would be?
a. Independent
b. Joint occurrence of events
c. Mutually exclusive
d. Complimentary probability

84. Correlation and regression analysis is used to determine the strength and direction of a linear relationship that exists between two continuous variables. Which of the following is NOT a use for correlation and regression analysis?
a. Prediction
b. Optimization
c. Explanation
d. Facilitation

85. The Cost of Poor Quality is the sum of internal and external failures and is made up of four cumulative area of costs. Which of the following is NOT a cost of poor quality?
a. Internal failure costs are costs that are caused by products or services not conforming to requirements or customer needs
b. Detection or the investment of it
c. Internal failure costs associated with initial production
d. Appraisal costs associated with finding defects

86. A green belt is calculating DPMO or Defects Per Million Opportunities. Using this information:

D is the number of defects
O is the number of opportunities for a defect
U is the number of units
TOP is the total number of opportunities = U times O
DPMO equals DPO times 1,000,000

Calculate the DPMO if:

D equals 15 total defects
O equals 5 opportunities or categories of defect types
U equals 10 pencils
TOP equals U times O equals 50 total opportunities

DPU equals D divided by TOP which equals 1.5 defects per unit or 15 total defects divided by 10 pencils.
DPO equals 0.30

a. DPMO equals 1,000
b. DPMO equals 300
c. DPMO equals 30,000
d. DPMO equals 300,000

87. The Gauge Repeatability and Reproducibility is the amount of measurement variation introduced by a measurement system and includes measuring the instrument itself and the individuals using the instrument. A Gauge R&R will quantify all of the following EXCEPT?
a. The level of significance
b. The combined effects of repeatability and reproducibility
c. Reproducibility which is the variation from the individuals using the instrument
d. Repeatability which is the variation from the measurement instrument

88. Which hypothesis test is used to test the difference of a sample mean x-bar with a known population mean and known population sigma?
a. One sample Z test
b. One sample
c. Two sample test
d. Paired t test

89. Which tool in the define phase shows a function of the factors of production and factors engineered into an operation so problems and barriers to quality and productivity are a function of malfunctioning factors of production engineered into an operation using the formula for this on the diagram is Y = F X?
a. Fishbone diagram
b. Pareto diagram
c. SIPOC diagram
d. High level process maps

90. A six sigma greenbelt is finalizing the project charter, determining the Voice of the Customer (VOC) determining the critical to quality elements CTQs and developing process metrics KPOVs. Which phase of the DMAIC methodology are they working?
a. Measure
b. Analyze
c. Define
d. Control

91. In project management which leadership style would be most aligned or used for teams which are self-directing?
a. Coaching
b. Directing
c. Supporting
d. Delegating

92. In 1987 the US Government introduced _____ presented annually by the president and designed to provide an operational definition of business excellence.
a. Military Standard MIL-STD-105A
b. The International Organization for Standardization (ISO)
c. The Malcolm Baldrige National Quality Award
d. Lean Six Sigma

93. Dr. Genichi Taguchi was a Japanese engineer and statistician whose work determined what product specification meant and how it could be applied to a cost effective production. Taguchi worked in just in time (JIT) production which is a production strategy that strives to improve a business return on investment by reducing in-process inventory and associated carrying costs. Taguchi product development includes three stages. Which of the following is NOT included?
a. Strategic planning
b. System design
c. Determining how the product should perform
d. Finding the balance between manufacturing unit cost profit and loss

94. The Plan-Do-Check-Act PDCA Cycle or Plan-Do-Study-Act PDCA cycle was invented by Shewhart but popularized by?
a. W. Edwards Deming
b. Carl Frederick Gauss
c. Joseph Juran
d. Genichi Taguchi

95. Which quality pioneer was credited with explaining how three sigma or three standard deviations is where a process needs to be corrected and that this is the point where a product will need to be remade because it will not pass a quality inspection?
a. Carl Frederick Gauss
b. Walter Shewart
c. W. Edwards Deming
d. Joseph Juran

96. Which representation is used to separate the "vital few" from the "trivial many" allowing the user to focus attention on a few important factors in a process?
a. Trend analyses
b. Scatter diagrams
c. Histograms
d. Pareto Diagrams

97. Which customer contact method would be used if a green belt wanted to confirm theories developed from other forms of customer contact?
a. Face to face interview
b. Survey
c. Focus group
d. Telephone interview

98. A value added analysis is used to determine what process steps customers are willing to pay for and those which they are not. The objectives of a value added and non-value added analysis include all of the following EXCEPT?
a. Identify hidden costs
b. Reduce process complexity
c. Reduce lead time
d. Reduce capacity

99. Which of the following tools would be best suited for improving the physical layout of a workspace?
a. Spaghetti diagram
b. SIPOC
c. Swim lane
d. Process map

100. Which of the following is not a proper use of brainstorming techniques?
a. Identify customers to include in research
b. Determine which phase of the DMAIC model to use
c. Identify which types of data to collect
d. Identify solution ideas

1. **The correct answer is (a)** The purpose of the Define phase of the six sigma methodology is to reach agreement on the scope, goals, and performance goals of a project. The deliverables of the define phase include a completed project charter, a high level process map, and completed project plans. It does not include a data collection plan. The data collection plan is developed under the measure phase.

2. **The correct answer is (d)** A SIPOC map will help identify Suppliers, Inputs, Process, Outputs, and customers. Observations is incorrect.

3. **The correct answer is (c)** The flowchart and value stream symbol which represents a decision point is ⬦ . represents electronic data system represents physical 💥 flow and represents project burst.

4. **The correct answer is (a)** The return on investment (ROI) is financial criteria used by executive management and project champions to determine whether to undergo a project in terms of costs of the project and benefits to the organization.

5. **The correct answer is (c)** The three key input components of quality are the customer, the employee, and the process. The value stream is not considered an input component of quality.

6. **The correct answer is (b)** 6. The pareto principle states that 20 percent of inputs result in 80 percent of outputs.

7. **The correct answer is (d)** A greenbelt would use a trend analysis to show if the improvements implemented in a project are improving from the baseline or benchmarks.

8. **The correct answer is (b)** When you know two variables are related it is not an appropriate application for a scatter diagram. The scatter diagram is used when you are trying to determine whether the two variables are related.

9. **The correct answer is (a)** The 1950's to 1960's represent Quality ERA 3 where quality assurance and good manufacturing practices are instituted.

10. **The correct answer is (c)** The 3rd Sigma level results in 66,807 defective parts per million, the 6th Sigma level only 3.4 defects per million opportunities, the 5th Sigma level 233 defective parts per million occur, the 4th Sigma level 6,210 defective parts per million occur.

11. **The correct answer is (b)** Eli Whitney developed interchangeable parts in 1798 for use in mass production. This invention allowed for interchangeable, reliable, standardized, organized parts.

12. **The correct answer is (b)** The stage of team development represented by team members becoming more comfortable and beginning to express their differences in opinion is storming.

The forming state of a project team is marked by uncertainty and tentativeness there may be anticipation by some team members. Team members are getting used to each other. The storming stage begins as the team members become more comfortable and begin to express their differences in opinion. In the norming the team rallies around their ability to meet the team objective. They communicate well and trust one another. At the performing stage team members begin to see tangible results and have a high level of interaction.

13. **The correct answer is (d)** Six Sigma Green Belts serve as a liaison between the Black Belts and the project team. They perform the operations required for the six sigma project and work with the project team ensuring that appropriate deliverables are met.

14. **The correct answer is (c)** The measure of central tendency where half the values are greater than or equal to it and half are less than or equal to it is the median. The mean is the average of a set of values. It is a measure of central tendency that is determined by adding all the values in a data set and dividing them by the total number of values. The mode is the most frequently occurring value in an array or range of data.

15. **The correct answer is (d)** The ratio measurement data scale would include measures such as height ages, weight, or length. Nominal data examines whether data are equivalent to a particular value such counts of coins. Ordinal data can be ranked but the differences between ordinal values cannot be quantified. Interval data has ordering with a constant scale but no natural zero.

16. **The correct answer is (c)** A Measurement Systems Analysis includes selecting the correct measurement and approach, assessing procedures and operators, and assessing the measuring device. It does not include determining the design of experiments. An experiment is typically designed to test a process but is not a step in an MSA.

17. **The correct answer is (b)** The more relaxed and wider the distribution the higher the Process Capability description of process capability is NOT correct. The correct statement would be the tighter or thinner the distribution the higher the Process Capability.

18. **The correct answer is (d)** Delivery is NOT an example of an external cost included in the costs of poor quality. Internal cost examples are, rework, delays, redesign, shortages, failure analysis, retesting, downtime and external cost examples are environmental costs, complaints, repairing goods and redoing services, customers' bad will, warranties, and sales losses.

19. **The correct answer is (a)** Values for correlation include 0 indicates no correlation, − 1 indicates a perfect negative correlation, and 1 indicates a perfect positive correlation. 0

indicates absolute correlation is incorrect. The value of r will always fall between –1 and 1.

20. **The correct answer is (b)** Timing ratio is incorrect this is the CR or Critical ratio which is an index number computed by dividing the time remaining until due date by the work time remaining.

21. **The correct answer is (c)** Using the statistical definition of the 95 percent confidence interval, if a poll of 100 people were taken 95 percent of respondents would be within the calculated confidence intervals and five percent would be either higher or lower than the range of the confidence intervals.

22. **The correct answer is (d)** The effects analysis part of an FMEA studies the consequences of the failures.

23. **The correct answer is (c)** Advancing the speed of a frozen dinner assembly is NOT an example of Poka Yoke application as it may improve efficiency and production but not quality in terms of preventing error.

24. **The correct answer is (a)** If the p Value is less than the alpha risk, reject the null hypothesis and accept the alternative hypothesis is NOT correct related to hypothesis acceptance. The correct statement is if the p Value is greater than the alpha risk, reject the null hypothesis and accept the alternative hypothesis.

25. **The correct answer is (b)** If a CEO were asking why printing costs are costing so much for a company and as the greenbelt you had reviewed paper costs, electricity costs, internal delivery costs, equipment rental costs, employee production costs using control charts and process charts
would be the most effective means of validating information.

26. **The correct answer is (b)**. Not identifying an important variable may cause special cause variation.

27. **The correct answer is (c)** If there are 4,261 defects per million opportunities, then the sigma level would be closest to 4 sigma. 2 sigma is 308,770 defects, 3 sigma is 66,811, 4 sigma is 6,210, 5 sigma is 233, and 5 sigma is 3.44

28. **The correct answer is (d)** The project charter justifies the project efforts with financial impact, defines roles of team members, describes the problem and scope but does not lists the tools to be used for the DMAIC.

29. **The correct answer is (c)** The main function of prototyping is to reduce project risk and cost.

30. **The correct answer is (b)** The X bar-s chart is used to plot the mean and standard deviation of a subgroup more than 5.

31. **The correct answer is (c)** A Spearman Rank Correlation coefficient be used for a measure that requires both variables be measured on an ordinal scale.

32. **The correct answer is (a)** In an FMEA the risk priority number is calculated by multiplying Severity x Occurrence x Detection.

33. **The correct answer is (d)** The analysis tool used to quantify the relationship between causes and effects would be the regression analysis.

34. **The correct answer is (a)** This formula denotes Cp process performance measure.

$$\frac{\text{Upper Specification Limit- Lower Specification Limit}}{6 \text{ x Process Standard Deviation}}$$

35. **The correct answer is (d)** Considering confidence intervals the width of the confidence interval decreases as the sample size increases.

36. **The correct answer is (b)** A process flow chart would BEST be used for determining the cause of delays in a process.

37. **The correct answer is (c)** The percentage of a product that completes processing on an assembly line without any additional work, repair or re-handling is the first pass yield. Work in process is work begun but not completed. Demand variation is the amount of fluctuation in the demand for the output of a process. Sigma capability is the rate of defects per defect opportunity.

38. **The correct answer is (a)** In lean six sigma Mura is unevenness in work and demand flow. Muri is having a greater demand than capacity in any given time or overburdening the process, series of processes or system. Muda waste has two types, type 1 is the necessary but non value adding waste. Type 2 is unnecessary, non-value adding waste.

39. **The correct answer is (d)** Equipment cost would NOT be considered a process metric. Is used to determine capital costs but not the cost of production.

40. **The correct answer is (a)** In the measure and control stages Poisson distribution would be used to estimate the number of instances of a condition occurring in a process or population.

41. **The correct answer is (c)** Statistical distributions can be characterized by all of the following parameters skewness, kurtosis, and central tendency. Congruency is not a statistical distribution characteristic.

42. **The correct answer is (d)** The diagram shows a negative correlation.

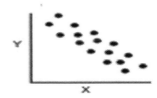

43. **The correct answer is (b)** If the points cluster in a band running from lower left to upper right, there is a positive correlation if x increases, y increases.

44. **The correct answer is (b)** The analysis which shows if the measurement system is equally accurate for large and small measurements and provides an indication of whether the bias error of a measurement system is constant throughout the range of equipment is linearity analysis.

45. **The correct answer is (d)** Multi-vari plots are used to assign variation to piece to piece variation, within piece or sample variation, time to time variation but not total variation.

46. **The correct answer is (b)** Stability component of measurement error is the capacity of a system to produce the same values over time on measurement of the same sample. Bias is a measure of the distance between the actual value and the average value of a part. Linearity measures the consistency of bias over the range of the measuring device. Accuracy is the degree of closeness to an expected mark.

47. **The correct answer is (a)** Total cycle time is NOT included in the calculation for a PERT analysis. Pessimistic time, optimistic time, and the most likely time are included.

48. **The correct answer is (d)** The process capability index shows with a single number if the process can meet the requirements of a customer.

49. **The correct answer is (c)** The six sigma tool pictured here that determines customer desires and what quality attributes the customer requires and groups the requirements that are critical in requirement by function, schedule, and performance is the house of quality.

50. **The correct answer is (c)** Simple linear regression is used when y is continuous and a single x variable exists. The residuals do not have to be negative but the following conditions must occur. The residuals have constant variance across all values of x, x can be ordinal or continuous, and the residuals are normally distributed.

51. **The correct answer is (a)** Computing the Mode, Mean, and Median of 5, 3, 23, 12, 8, 14, 29, and 24 results in Mode= none, Mean=14.75 Median=14.

52. **The correct answer is (b)** These two formulas are used to calculate upper and lower control limits.

$$UCL_p = \bar{p} + 3\sqrt{\frac{\bar{p}(1-\bar{p})}{n}}$$

$$LCL_p = \bar{p} - 3\sqrt{\frac{\bar{p}(1-\bar{p})}{n}}$$

53. **The correct answer is (a)** A run of four in a row on the same side of the centerline is NOT an indication of an out-

of-control signal in a control chart with a sample of 20 at least 8 should be on the same side of the center line.

54. **The correct answer is (d)** Variation is a change in data, characteristic, or function caused by one of four factors. Social variation is NOT one of the four factors causing variation. The four factors include special causes, tampering, common causes, and structural variation.

55. **The correct answer is (d)** Deming offered fourteen key principles to management for transforming business effectiveness. Some of the key points include: Create constancy of purpose toward improvement, adopt the new philosophy, accept change, the lowest cost isn't always the best, improve constantly, institute training on the job, institute good leadership do what you say, say what you do and put everyone in the company to work to accomplish the transformation.

56. **The correct answer is (a)** The method for keeping a process within boundaries or the act of minimizing the variation of a process is called process control.

57. **The correct answer is (a)** ISO 9001 is the set of International Standards Organization (ISO) standards that covers quality management and quality assurance.

58. **The correct answer is (c)** Recycle Cost is NOT included in the cost of quality or the costs associated with providing poor quality product or service. The four elements include: External Failure Cost, Internal Failure Cost, Inspection (appraisal) Cost, and Prevention Cost.

59. **The correct answer is (b).** Deming's theories and his System of Profound Knowledge consisted of four interrelated parts. The Theory of Optimization, Theory of Variation, Theory of Knowledge, and Theory of Psychology. The theory of Analysis is NOT included.

60. **The correct answer is (d)** DMADV is a Six Sigma quality initiative for designing products and processes. The steps in the DMADV model are define, measure, analyze, design and verify.

61. **The correct answer is (d)** Taiichi Ohno studied wastes and its impact on quality under his teachings there are eight forms of waste. 1. overproduction ahead of demand 2. waiting for the next process 3. unnecessary transport of materials 4. over-processing of parts 5. inventories more than the minimum 6. unnecessary movement by employees 7. production of defective parts and 8. under-utilization of employees talent.

62. **The correct answer is (c)** A quality metric that asks a question such as how many billing errors occurred in the last billing cycle is an example of discrete data.

63. **The correct answer is (b)** A dataset positive correlation would have all of the following implications, the independent variable decreases as the dependent variable

increases, the dependent variable decreases as the independent variable increases, and the dependent variable improves as the independent variable increases but would not include the dependent variable increases as the independent variable increases.

64. **The correct answer is (a)** A dataset negative correlation would have all of the following implications the dependent variable increases as the independent variable increases, the independent variable decreases as the dependent variable decreases, and the dependent variable improves as the independent variable decreases but would not include the dependent variable decreases as the independent variable increases.
.

65. **The correct answer is (d)** The Pareto principle defined by J. M. Juran states that most effects come from relatively few causes. It shows 80% of the effects come from 20% of the possible causes.

66. **The correct answer is (a)** A quality tool used for collecting and analyzing data on the frequency or patterns of events, problems, defects, defect location, defect causes, particularly in production processes is the check sheet.

67. **The correct answer is (d)** The six sigma tool used to improve a teams creativity and thinking developed by Jiro Kawakita which organizes a large number of ideas into their natural relationships is the affinity diagram.

68. **The correct answer is (c)** The analyze phase of the DMAIC model includes determining where problems or defects occur. In the define phase you determine what problem needs to be solved. In the measure phase you determine the capabilities of your processes. In the improve phase you determine how your processes can be improved and implement trials of your solutions. In the control phase you determine what can be put into place to sustain the improvements you have made.

69. **The correct answer is (a)** Given a cost savings of $624,584, investment of $228,330 and labor of $42,638 the ROI is 2.30 calculated by $624,584/ ($228,330 + $42,638)

70. **The correct answer is (d)** When working with probability theory, an expression or string of symbols intended to represent a numerical value must follow commonly accepted and unambiguous rules is called the order of operators.

71. **The correct answer is (a)** Determining benchmarks is NOT a step in testing a hypothesis.

72. **The correct answer is (b)** A chart in which the critical work elements of a project are illustrated to portray their relationships to each other and to the project as a whole allowing the project manager predict outcomes based on various scenarios and ensuring optimum decisions are made about whether or not to adopt suggested procedures or changes is the Work Breakdown Structure (WBS).

73. **The correct answer is (d)** Closed-Loop Analysis is a formal business intelligence process intended to set business goals, monitor progress, assess impact or effectiveness and then realign objectives. It becomes a real-time process when data is collected and evaluated continuously refined. It does not align the resources.

74. **The correct answer is (b)** An ethical balance cannot be created from a balanced scorecard. Alignment of individual and corporate objectives, culture driven by performance, and support of shareholder value creation are benefits of the balanced scorecard.

75. **The correct answer is (c)** Means display average to the norm not the total combined effects of the data.

76. **The correct answer is (a)** Goldratt developed the Theory of Constraints that organizations can be measured and controlled by variations on three measures which include throughput, operating expense, and inventory, it does not include employee motivation.

77. **The correct answer is (d)** Total Productive Maintenance (TPM) is a Japanese management philosophy used to increase time between failure (MTBF) or life of machinery. VOC is the voice of the customer, Theory of Constraints (TOC) is a special sequence which is claimed to deliver higher results than if each one of the continuous methodologies were used individually. Cost-Time-Resource (CTR) determines workload and resource requirements.

78. **The correct answer is (d)** The residuals are independent not dependent and the residuals are normally distributed, X can be ordinal or continuous, and the residuals have constant variance across all values of x.

79. **The correct answer is (b)** DPU represents the number of defects divided by the number of products. Quality Function Deployment (QFD) is a systematic process for motivating a business to focus on its customers. It is used by cross-functional teams to identify and resolve issues involved in providing products, processes, services and strategies which will more than satisfy their customers. Cost of poor COPQ quality allows the organization to analyze wastes Cost of Poor Quality allows you to get an estimate of these wastes and speak the language of management in terms of it. DPMO refers to defects per million opportunities in process improvement it is a measure of process performance. It is defined as 1,000,000 multiplied by the number of defects divided by the number of units multiplied by the number of opportunities per unit.

80. **The correct answer is (b)** The data collection plan is NOT a tool used in determining the project scope.

81. **The correct answer is (d)** A type of bar chart that illustrates a project schedule with start and finish dates of the terminal elements and summary elements of a project

including the work breakdown structure and the dependency of relationships between activities would be the Gantt chart.

82. **The correct answer is (d)** A data analysis technique for determining if a measurement process has gone out of statistical control and is sensitive to changes in the number of defective items in the measurement process would be the C chart.

83. **The correct answer is (b)** If it is impossible for two events to occur together these would be
mutually exclusive.

84. **The correct answer is (d)** Correlation and regression analysis is used to determine prediction of the production volume of a process, explanation of costs, and optimization of customer relationship strength. Facilitation is not included.

85. **The correct answer is (c)** Internal failure costs associated with initial production is NOT a cost of poor quality. The fourth cost is external failure costs that are caused by deficiencies found after delivery of products and services to external customers.

86. **The correct answer is (d)** If a green belt is calculating DPMO or Defects Per Million Opportunities. Using this information:

D is the number of defects
O is the number of opportunities for a defect
U is the number of units
TOP is the total number of opportunities = U times O
DPMO equals DPO times 1,000,000

DPO equals 0.30 times 1,000,000 which equals 300,000 out of a million opportunities, the long term performance of the process would create 300,000 defects.

87. **The correct answer is (a)** A gauge R&R will quantify reproducibility which is the variation from the individuals using the instrument, repeatability which is the variation from the measurement instrument, and the combined effects of repeatability and reproducibility. It does not quantify the level of significance.

88. **The correct answer is (a)** A one sample Z test is used to test the difference of a sample mean x-bar with a known population mean and known population sigma.

89. **The correct answer is (a)** A Fishbone diagram is a tool in the define phase which shows a function of the factors of production and factors engineered into an operation so problems and barriers to quality and productivity are a function of malfunctioning factors of production engineered into an operation using the formula for this on the diagram is Y = F X.

90. **The correct answer is (c)** A six sigma greenbelt is working in the Define phase of the six sigma methodology if they are finalizing the project charter, determining the Voice of the Customer VOC determining the critical to quality elements CTQs and developing process metrics KPOVs.

91. **The correct answer is (d)** In project management the delegating leadership style would be most aligned or used for teams which are self-directing. Delegating is useful for teams which are empowered and self-directing. Supporting leadership style is used for teams that require continual support in terms of competencies and experience. Coaching is used for those teams on the verge of being self-directed. Directing leadership is used for teams which are new or on time sensitive projects.

92. **The correct answer is (c)** In 1987 the US Government introduced the Malcolm Baldrige National Quality Award presented annually by the president and designed to provide an operational definition of business excellence.

93. **The correct answer is (a)** Taguchi product development includes three stages system design, determining how the product should perform, and finding the balance between manufacturing unit cost profit and loss.

94. **The correct answer is (a)** The Plan-Do-Check-Act PDCA Cycle or Plan-Do-Study-Act PDCA cycle was invented by Shewhart but popularized by W. Edwards Deming.

95. **The correct answer is (b)** Walter Shewart was credited with explaining how three sigma or three standard deviations is where a process needs to be corrected and that this is the point where a product will need to be remade because it will not pass a quality inspection.

96. **The correct answer is (d)** Pareto Diagrams are used to separate the "vital few" from the "trivial many" allowing the user to focus attention on a few important factors in a process.

97. **The correct answer is (b)** If a green belt wanted to confirm theories developed from other forms of customer contact they would use the survey form of customer contact method.

98. **The correct answer is (d)** The objectives of a value added and non-value added analysis include identifying hidden costs, reducing process complexity, and reducing lead time. Reducing capacity is not correct you actually want to improve or increase capacity.

99. **The correct answer is (a)** A spaghetti diagram would be best suited for improving the physical layout of a workspace.

100. **The correct answer is (b)** The choice of "determine which phase of the DMAIC model to use" is NOT a proper use of brainstorming techniques. The phases are distinct in function and do not require brainstorming to determine which phase to use.

Conclusion

Now that you have a firm understanding of the exam and what is included in our study guide, don't forget that learning how to be a great test taker can be just as important as learning the content on the exam. Trivium Test Prep is offering a **FREE *Six Sigma Green Belt Essential Test Tips*** DVD. Our DVD includes 35 test preparation strategies that will make you successful on the Six Sigma Green Belt. All we ask is that you email us your feedback and describe your experience with our product. Amazing, awful, or just so-so: we want to hear what you have to say!

To receive your **FREE *Six Sigma Green Belt Essential Test Tips*** DVD, please email us at 5star@triviumtestprep.com. Include
"Free 5 Star" in the subject line and the following information in your email:

1. The title of the product you purchased.

2. Your rating from 1 – 5 (with 5 being the best).

3. Your feedback about the product, including how our materials helped you meet your goals and ways in which we can improve our products.

4. Your full name and shipping address so we can send your FREE *Six Sigma Green Belt Essential Test Tips* DVD.

Thank you!

-

Made in the USA
Lexington, KY
30 June 2019